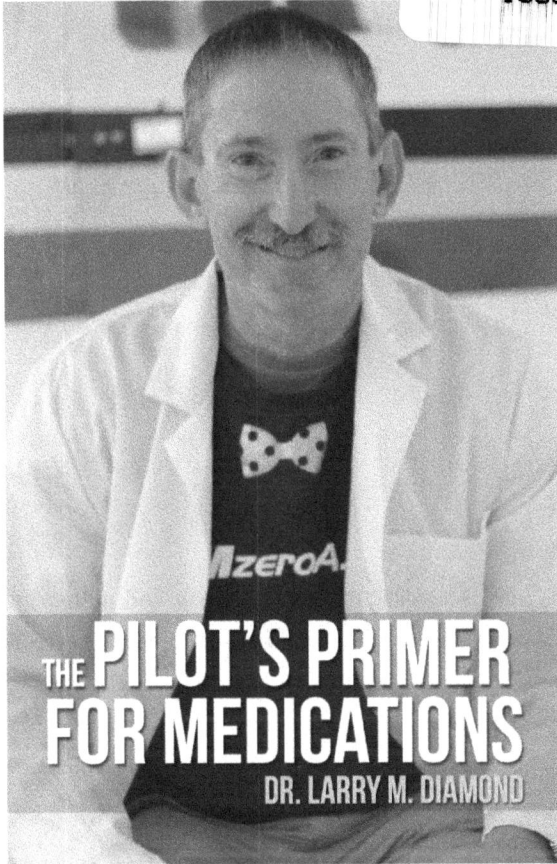

THE PILOT'S PRIMER FOR MEDICATIONS

DR. LARRY M. DIAMOND

Dr Larry M. Diamond PharmD

ISBN-13: 978-0692248140 (MzeroA.com)

ISBN-10: 0692248145

This publication is designed to provide accurate and authoritative information in regard to the subject matter covered. However nothing in this book supersedes any operational documents or FAA regulations. This book is sold with the understanding that the neither publisher nor the author is liable for any damages caused or alleged to be caused directly, indirectly, incidentally, or consequentially by the information in this book.

Proudly printed in the United States of America

Disclaimer

The database that is utilized is compiled by the AOPA Medical Certification Department and is based upon confirmation with the FAA Aerospace Medical Certification Division in Oklahoma City. Although these medications are generally allowed by the FAA for flight duties, there are variables with each individual's situation that could render a particular medication inappropriate for flying because of case history or adverse side effects. Some medications are being used "off label". This means that a drug is prescribed for symptoms that do not fall within the FDA's approval guidelines for that drug. This is just one example of why the FAA might not approve a drug that is on the list.

FAR 61.53 prohibits a person from acting as pilot in command or as a required pilot flight crew member while that person (1) "knows or has reason to know of any medical condition that would make the person unable to meet the requirements for the medical certificate necessary for the pilot operation"; or, (2) "Is taking medication or receiving other treatment for a medical condition that results in the person being unable to meet the requirements for the medical certificate necessary for the pilot operation."

FAR 91.17 states (a) No person may act or attempt to act as a pilot crew member of a civil aircraft...

> (3) While using any drug that affects the person's faculties in any way contrary to safety...

Although we maintain the medications list as accurately as possible, there may be drugs that do not appear in the database. If you have any questions about a particular medication that does not appear, contact the Medical

Certification specialists on the AOPA Pilot Information Center, 800/872-2672.

Do not consider the content as medical advice. Never delay or disregard seeking professional medical advice from your doctor or other qualified healthcare provider because of something you have read. You should always speak with your doctor before you start, stop, or change any prescribed part of your care plan or treatment. This resource or others obtainable via the media or on the internet should ever be a substitute for professional medical advice, diagnosis, or treatment from a qualified health care provider. If you think you may have a medical emergency, call your doctor or dial 911 immediately.

Chapter 4 61

Chapter 5 80

Chapter 6 85

About The Author

I have been flying since 1984. I received my Private Pilot Certificate, October 23, 1984, Instrument rating, July 1992, Commercial rating August 2005, CFI, March 6, 2007 1620 EST (2120Z), and CFII, June 30, 2013, 1345 EDT (1745Z). I am a Flight Instructor at Solo Aviation, Ann Arbor, MI (KARB) and Instructor in Command at MzeroA.com

Education and Affiliation: B.S. Zoology, Michigan State University 1974, B.S. Pharmacy Wayne State University 1980, Doctor of Pharmacy, Idaho State University 2002, Cardiac Associate, American College of Cardiology.

Employment: Clinical Pharmacy Specialist - Cardiology, Oakwood Hospital - Dearborn, Dearborn, MI.

Dedication

I dedicate this book to my best friend and wife of 33 years, Yvonne, my wonderful son Andrew, my late son Mike who we lost too soon that I learned so much from, my Golden Doodle Maya, Solo Aviation and my wonderful friends from MzeroA.com, Jason and Ashley Schappert who have given me the opportunity to share my aviation knowledge, teach students and pilots from all over the world and experience a caring mission and passion to train pilots in an unique and state of the art method.

Forward By Rod Machado:

Anyone who has earned a pilot certificate is intimately familiar with the cost of that endeavor. You invest your time and money—large blocks of daylight hours spread out over many months and literally thousands of dollars—to earn the privilege of taking a flying machine into the air. Your watch and wallet, however, say nothing about the blood, sweat, and tears involved in this enterprise. You had to overcome frustration, confusion, and self-doubt as you learned to move a piston-powered conveyance safely from one airport to the next. Congratulations to you! Yours is a magnificent accomplishment.

Now hear this. Everything that you earned and learned can be taken away from you instantly by putting the wrong little pill in your mouth.

That's right. Take an unapproved medication (one that's not sanctioned by the FAA), and your friendly aviation medical examiner (AME) suddenly becomes the repo man. As a representative of the FAA, the good doctor is obliged to repossess (so to speak) your medical certification to act as pilot in command because you no longer meet the FAA's standards. Sure, you might eventually reclaim your medical certificate, but not without further investment of your time and money. There may be a pain pill big enough to assuage the headache this causes, but there's no way to swallow it.

In an ideal world, this wouldn't matter much. Your AME would tell you to go back to your physician, have him or her prescribe a drug that's approved by the FAA, then return to pick up your medical certificate. No muss, no fuss, no extensive and expensive FAA involvement. Unfortunately, the only place on earth where this "commonsense" approach could happen is in Fantasyland at the Disneyland theme park.

Ultimately, you are responsible for knowing what medications or medical procedures are acceptable to the FAA for the maladies that affect you. Until now, it was a megaorder challenge to identify these medications. Here is where fortune smiles on you. My friend, Dr. Larry Diamond's new book, *The Pilot's Primer for Prescription Medications*, is the resource that should be in every pilot's library, if not flight bag.

Dr. Diamond's book is the pilot's practical resource for prescription medication. It's easy to navigate, easy to read, and easy to use. It's your initial source for identifying the medications that the FAA considers acceptable at this point in time. So prepare for your next medical examination by reading Dr. Diamond's book now, not later. Make sure the medications you're taking (if any) or are planning on taking are on the FAA's approved list. If not, do something about it before your AME does.

Following the advice put forth in this valuable book will keep you from being unpleasantly surprised during your next visit to the AME. Take it from me—Dr. Larry Diamond knows what he is talking about. He's a master of medical molecules whose informative new book will keep you airworthy for many years to come.

Rod Machado
San Clemente,
June 10th 2014

Purpose and Objective

Pilots at some point, during their flying careers will be prescribed medication/s for a short or chronic period of time. All medications have a huge list of side effects and will affect the pathophysiology of pilots in individual ways. The pilot should always go through their IMSAFE checklist before each flight. The M for medications is sometimes overlooked by the pilot. Each medication that is prescribed by the physician or is being taken over the counter has a purpose to alleviate or control symptoms from a disease state.

My purpose and objective is to educate, in a general overview how these medications work and why they are being prescribed. I will incorporate the FAA's guidelines for some of the most common disease states, what medications are commonly used and then list medications that have been deemed safe to take per the FAA Approved Safe Medication list as put together by AOPA.

As stated above, I will speak on some of the most common over the counter medications and how by themselves may affect the flight to be taken and how they may interact with prescription medications. I will start with what medications will prevent an applicant, when going for their appointment with the AME from getting a Medical Certificate for pilot training or when renewing their medical certificate.

As mentioned in the disclaimer, this reference book is to give an applicant or pilot a good general overview and foundation in understanding the medications they take on a daily basis. Any questions on an individual basis should be directed to your physician.

Chapter 1

Medications that will *Prevent* you from obtaining a FAA Medical Certificate.

The biggest medical category that will disqualify an applicant in pursuit of a medical certificate is psychiatric disorders. Personality disorders that manifest overt acts, psychosis with delusions, hallucinations, bizarre, disorganized behavior, bipolar disorder, substance dependency including alcohol, opioids, cocaine, sedatives, hypnotics, cannabis, psychoactive drugs and substance abuse within the preceding 2 years are all disqualifying reasons for obtaining a medical certificate. So along with these psychiatric disease states, any of the medications that treat the previously mentioned areas would also be disqualifications for a medical certificate.

Background

Under Title 14 of the Code of Federal Regulations (14 CFR) 67.107(c), 67.207(c), and 67.307(c) and 67.113(c), 67.213(c) and 67.313 (c), the FAA generally considers a diagnosis of depression and use of psychotropic medication medically disqualifying for applicants for FAA medical

certification. Disqualifying medication generally includes all sedatives, tranquilizers, antipsychotics,

antidepressants **(including selective serotonin reuptake inhibitors (SSRIs {until 2010 see below}))**, analeptics, anxiolytics, and hallucinogens. Aviation Medical Examiners (AMEs) defer medical certificate issuance for any applicant with a disqualifying medical condition, including any applicant who reveals on a medical certificate application usage of psychotropic medication for treatment of depression.

FAA Do Not Issue - Do Not Fly
Guide for Aviation Medical Examiners

The information in this section is provided to advise Aviation Medical Examiners (AMEs) about two medication issues:

Medications for which they should not issue applicants without clearance from the Federal Aviation Administration (FAA), AND

Medications for which for which they should advise airmen to not fly and provide additional safety information to the applicant.

The lists of medications in this section are not meant to be all-inclusive or comprehensive, but rather address the most common concerns.

Do Not Issue. AMEs should not issue airmen medical certificates to applicants who are using these medications. If there are any questions, please call the Regional Flight Surgeon's office or the Aerospace Medicine Certification Division.

• Anticholinergics (oral)

• Antiseizure medications, even if used for non-seizure conditions

• Centrally acting antihypertensives, including but not limited to clonidine,

reserpine, guanethidine, guanadrel, guanabenz, and methyldopa

•   Bromocriptine

• Dopamine agonists used for Parkinson's disease or other medical indications: Pramipexole (Mirapex), ropinirole (Requip) and rotigotine (NeuPro). All carry warnings for suddenly falling asleep during activities of daily living

• Mefloquine (Lariam)

- Over-active bladder medications. Almost all of these medications are antimuscarinic. Antimuscarinic medications carry strong warnings about potential for sedation and impaired cognition

  - Varenicline (Chantix)

- An open prescription for regular or intermittent use of any drug or substance classified under the Controlled Substances Act (Schedules I – V).

This includes medical marijuana, even if legally allowed or prescribed under state law.

Note: exceptions would be for documented temporary use of the drug solely for a medical procedure or for a medical condition, and the medication has been discontinued.

- Most psychiatric or psychotropic medications, including but not limited to antipsychotics, most antidepressants (see SSRI policy), antianxiety drugs, mood stabilizers, attention deficit disorder (ADD) or attention deficit hyperactivity disorder (ADHD) medications, sedative-hypnotics and tranquilizers

- High doses of oral steroids (greater than 20 mg prednisone or prednisone- equivalent per day)

- Agents for treating cancer, including chemotherapeutics, biologics, etc., whether used for induction, "maintenance," or suppressive therapy

- Antiangina medications

- Concurrent use of a beta-blocker plus a sulfonylurea or insulin or a meglitinide. Commonly used meglitinides include repaglinide (Prandin) and nateglinide (Starlix). Commonly used sulfonylureas include: acetohexamide (Dymelor); chloropropamide (Diabinese); tolazamide (Tolinase); tolbutamide (Orinase); glimepiride (Amaryl); glipizide (Glucotrol, Glucotrol XL); glyburide (DiaBeta, Micronase, Glynase); glyburide plus metformin (Glucovance); glipizide plus metformin (Metaglip)

- Any medication newly approved by the Food and Drug Administration (FDA) (those drugs issued initial FDA marketing approval within the past 12 months). We require at least one-year of post-marketing experience with a new drug before we will consider whether we can safely certificate an applicant using the drug. New antibiotics, lipid-lowering drugs, and antihypertensive medications can be considered earlier than one year. Please contact the RFS or AMCD for guidance on specific applicants.

Do Not Fly

•Airmen should not fly while using any of the medications in the **Do Not Issue** section above or using any of the medications or classes/groups of medications listed below. All of these medications below may cause sedation (drowsiness) or impair cognitive function, seriously degrading pilot performance. This impairment can occur even when the individual feels alert and is apparently functioning normally – in other words, the airman can be "unaware of impair."

For aviation safety, airmen should not fly following the last dose of any of the medications below until a period of time has elapsed equal to:

- 5-times the maximum pharmocologic half life of the medication; or

- 5-times the maximum hour dose interval **if** pharmacologic half-life information is not available. For example, there is a 30-hour wait time for a medication that is taken every 4 to 6 hours (5 times 6)

Sleep aids. All the currently available sleep aids, both prescription and over-the-counter (OTC), can cause impairment of mental processes and reaction times, even when the individual feels fully awake.

- Diphenhydramine (e.g., Benadryl). Many OTC sleep aids contain diphenhydramine as the active ingredient. The wait time after diphenhydramine is 60 hours (based on maximum pharmacologic half life)

  Allergy medications. Antihistamines found in many allergy and other types of medications can cause sedation and may **not** be used for flight. This applies to nasal formulations as well as oral.

Exception: Nonsedating antihistamines (loratadine, desloratadine, and fexofenadine) may be used while flying, if symptoms are controlled without adverse side effects after an adequate initial trial period.

Label warnings. Airmen should not fly while using any medication, prescription or OTC, that carries a label precaution or warning that **it may cause drowsiness or advises the user "be careful when driving a motor vehicle or operating machinery."** This applies even if label states "until you know how the medication affects you" and even if the airman has used the medication before with no apparent adverse effect. Such medications can cause impairment even when the airman feels alert and unimpaired (see "unaware of impair" above).

"Pre-medication" or "pre-procedure" drugs. This includes all drugs used as an aid to outpatient surgical or dental procedures.

Narcotic pain relievers. This includes but is not limited to morphine, codeine, oxycodone

(Percodan; Oxycontin), and hydrocodone (Vicodin, etc.).

Muscle relaxants. This includes but is not limited to carisoprodol (Soma) and cyclobenzaprine (Flexeril).

Over-the-counter active dietary supplements such as Kava-Kava and Valerian.

Wow, that is a lot of things that will keep the pilot from flying. I agree, but if a medication/s will impair the pilots ability to perform at 100%, that pilot should not be flying. Be it the side effect, of drowsiness, inability to concentrate, headache, diarrhea, double vision and hypertension, this is not the mental and physical state a pilot should be in before a flight. With 8 hours of sleep, a great breakfast, healthy lifestyle and a safe, current and proficient pilot, the decisions will be made while flying, will be in a very clear, fast and concise manner. Anything that will impair this should be a NO-GO.

Examples of <u>medications</u> in this category that would disqualify an applicant
(You will see two names for each medication, 1) Trade name and 2) Chemical or generic name)

1. **Abilify** (aripiprazole) - antispychotic
2. **Elavil** (amitriptyline) - antidepressant
3. **Anafranil** (clomipramine) - antidepressant
4. **Ativan** (lorazepam) - antianxiety
5. **Buspar** (buspirone) - antianxiety
6. **Klonopin** (clonazepam) - antianxiety
7. **Clozaril** (clozapine) - antipsychotic
8. **Cymbalta** (duloxetine) - antidepressant
9. **Desyrel** (trazodone) - antidepressant
10. **Sinequan** (doxepin) - antidepressant
11. **Effexor** (venlafaxine) - antidepressant
12. **Eskalith** (lithium carbonate) - bipolar medications
13. **Haldol** (haloperidol) - antipsychotic
14. **Librium** (chlordiazepoxide) - antianxiety
15. **Loxitane** (loxapine) - antipsychotic
16. **Luvox** (fluvoxamine) - antidepressant
17. **Pamelor** (nortriptyline) - antidepressant
18. **Paxil** (paroxetine) - antidepressant
19. **Remeron** (mirtazapine) - antipsychotic
20. **Seroquel** (quetiapine) - antipsychotic
21. **Serzone** (nefazodone) - antidepressant

22. **Surmontil** (trimipramine) - antidepressant

23. **Tofranil** (imipramine) - antidepressant

24. **Tranxene** (clorazepate dipotassium) - antianxiety

25. **Valium** (diazepam) - antianxiety

26. **Wellbutrin and Zyban** (bupropion) - antidepressant

27. **Xanax** (alprazolam) - antianxiety

28. **Zyprexa** (olanzapine) - antipsychotic

The psychiatric disease states mentioned involve folks who have problems coping, hallucinating, having delusions, seeing and hearing people who do not exist. They cannot sleep, do not realize where they are, do not want to eat and are not doing their normal daily tasks. They are having problems just getting out of bed and dealing with life. You can easily see why the FAA doesn't want to have people who are going through this in a cockpit. If you cannot cope with life on the ground you definitely can not cope with what is happening in an aircraft at 3,000 feet.

Each of the above medications can cause a majority of side effects that affect the cognition of the patient. There are also some very toxic side effects that could cause death. Everyone of the above medications will in some degree cause drowsiness. This is a side effect that by itself will cause a no-go decision even if not on a medications. Many of the atypical antipsychotics, such as **Zyprexa®, Seroquel®, Remeron®** and **Cymbalta®** have a potential to cause life threatening cardiac arrhythmias called ventricular tachycardia. This arrhythmia will cause the bottom chamber of the heart, called the ventricle to beat over 300 beats per minute. The heart is quivering and it is literally dead. These same medications could also cause a patient to have extrapyramidal side effects like tardive dyskinesia which include involuntary repetitive body movements, grimacing, lip smacking, excessive eye blinking and torticollis (abnormal twisting of the neck).

With the benzodiazepines, such as **Xanax®** and **Ativan®**, drowsiness and lethargy are common side effects. **Wellbutrin®** and **Zyban®** at very high doses could cause seizures. All are big reasons why the FAA have deemed these medications as not safe to fly on.

<u>Good News</u> for patients who have had depression on 4 particular SSRI's

In April of 2010, the FAA determined that airmen requesting first, second, or third class medical certificates while being treated with 4 particular selective serotonin reuptake inhibitors (SSRI) may be considered for Special Issuance (SI). Also if applicants have been off an SSRI for 60 days with a favorable report from the treating physician and they indicate a stable mood and no aeromedical side effects, they also can apply for a SI.

The applicant must have the following diagnoses: 1) major depressive disorder (mild to moderate), 2) Dysthymic disorder, 3) Adjustment Disorder with a depressed mood or 4) any non-depression related condition that an SSRI is being used. The applicant must be on the designated SSRI continuously for at least 12 months and be on a stable dose without aeromedically significant side effects. The 4 SSRI's include: **Prozac®** (fluoxetine), **Zoloft®** (sertraline), **Celexa®** (citalopram), and **Lexapro®** (escitalopram). The SSRI's have a long track record for working in depression 80-90% of the time.

FAA PHARMACEUTICAL CONSIDERATIONS

The use of a psychotropic drug is disqualifying for aeromedical certification purposes – this includes all antidepressant drugs, including selective serotonin reuptake inhibitors (SSRIs). However, the FAA has determined that airmen requesting first, second, or third class medical certificates while being treated with one of four specific SSRIs may be considered (see Item 47., Psychiatric Conditions – Use of Antidepressant Medications). The Autorization decision is made on a case by case basis. **The Examiner may not issue.**

How do SSRI's Work

Serotonin is produced in the brain. It is a neurotransmitter that helps transfer messages from one part of the brain to another. Serotonin affects mood, brain function, appetite, sleep, memory and learning, temperature regulation, sexual desire and social behavior. The best thing would be for serotonin to floating around in our brains at a consistent level. Serotonin needs storage sites. If there is an imbalance due lack of production, lack of receptor sites and an inability to reach the receptor sites, a change in mental state could occur. Low levels may lead to depression, anxiety and panic. SSRI's will prevent the reuptake of serotonin, which will increase the levels in the brain if low.

Other medications that will prevent an applicant a medical certificate

The biggest group are particular oral anti-cancer medications. A few examples are:

1. **Zytiga** (abiraterone) - prostate cancer
2. **Yervoy** (ipilimumab) - melanoma
3. **Velcade** (bortezomib) - multiple myeloma
4. **Trelstar** (triptoreline) - prostate cancer
5. **Tarceva** (erlotinib) - small cell lung cancer
6. **Sutent** (sunitibib) - renal cell cancer
7. **Revlimid** (lenalidomide) - multiple myeloma

8. **Nexavar** (sorafenib) - renal cell cancer

9. **Firmagon** (degarelix) - prostate cancer

10. **Avastin** (bevacizumab) - metastatic colon cancer

Diabetic Medications not on the safe to take list

1. **Bydureon XR** (exaneatide) - injectable antihyperglycemic

2. **Invokana** (canagliflozin) - antihyperglycemic

3. **Symlin -** (pramlintide) - injectable antihyperglycemic

4. **Takeda -** (alogliptin) - diabetes type II (people that have low amounts of insulin or do not work well)

Cardiac Medications

1. **Imdur** (nitroglycerin) - vasodilator antiischemic (prevents chest pain)

2. **Brilinta** (ticagrelor) - antiplatelet

3. **Pradaxa** (dabigatran) - anticoagulant

4. **Eliquis** (apixaban) - anticoagulant

Over the Counter (OTC) medications not on the safe list

1. **Benadryl** (diphenhydramine) - antihistamine and used for sleep

2. **Dramamine** (dimenhydrinate) - motion sickness

All of the anticonvulsants, ADHD and narcolepsy, muscle relaxant, migraine, OTC sleeper (**Unisom**), urinary antispasmotic, pain (**Vicodin, Morphine and Codeine**) medications are NOT on the list.

If you are smoking......QUIT and if you are trying to quit, do not use **Chantix** (varenicline). **Chantix** has had reports to the FDA of causing abnormal behavior and suicidal intentions.

Chapter 2
Hypertension

Hypertension is having an elevated blood pressure. Hypertension has been labeled, "The Silent Killer." I visualize pipes and water when thinking about hypertension. A nice big pipe with an adequate amount of water moving through is normal blood pressure. Same amount of water going through a smaller diameter pipe is high blood pressure. Higher amount of water going through a normal sized pipe is high blood pressure also. Blood pressure is measured by two numbers, systolic blood pressure and diastolic blood pressure.

The top number is systolic pressure which is the pressure in the bottom chamber of the heart as it pumps blood out. Diastolic is the pressure in bottom chamber when the blood is filling. People with hypertension feel pretty good because blood from the heart is being delivered to the brain, eyes, kidneys and peripheral organs in a very forceful way. Sounds good, except that hypertension causes heart disease, kidney dysfunction, stroke, hemorrhages in the eye and atherosclerosis (accumulation of cholesterol in the vessels). The atherosclerosis cause plaques to form in the arteries that sit on top of the heart.

These coronary arteries supply blood to the heart muscle. In the face of inflammation the plaques will bust and form clot that will clog a coronary artery. This will lead to a heart attack. A person's weight plays a major role in hypertension. Loss of 10% of body weight will lead to a 10% decrease in blood pressure. Exercise and a decrease in dietary salt intake will also decrease blood pressure.

This is the FAA's disposition for Hypertension and Hypertension Medications:

If an individual with no known history of hypertension is found, during the FAA exam to have blood pressure readings consistently higher than 155/95 then further investigation is required. Initially, this should consist of recording the blood pressure twice a day (morning and evening) for three consecutive days. If at least 4 of these 6 readings are 155/95 or less and the applicant is otherwise qualified, then no further action is required and the certificate can be issued.

PHARMACEUTICAL CONSIDERATIONS

- Medications acceptable to the FAA for treatment of hypertension in airmen include all Food and Drug Administration (FDA) approved diuretics, alpha-adrenergic blocking agents, beta-adrenergic blocking agents, calcium channel blocking agents, angiotensin converting enzyme (ACE inhibitors) agents, and direct vasodilators.

- **NOT** acceptable to the FAA:

Centrally acting agents (such as reserpine, guanethidine, guanadrel, guanabenz, and methyldopa).

A combination of beta-adrenergic blocking agents used with insulin, meglitinides, or sulfonylureas.

- The Examiner must **defer** issuance of a medical certificate to any applicant whose hypertension has not been evaluated, who uses **unacceptable** medications, whose medical status is unclear, whose hypertension is uncontrolled, who manifests significant adverse effects of medication, or whose certification has previously been specifically reserved to the FAA.

Acceptable FAA medications, Hypertension Medication Categories and how they work

Angiotensin Converting Enzyme Inhibitors (ACEI) - This type of medication works on multiple pathways in the body. The body has many processes to increase blood pressure if it senses a low blood pressure. When the body stays hypertensive it really revs up these pathways. The kidneys will release a substance called renin which is a vasoconstrictor. Another enzyme will be released called angiotensinogen and be converted to angiotensin I, another vasoconstrictor. Angiotensin I gets converted to Angiotensin II, another vasoconstrictor. Angiotensin II is a more potent vasocontrictor than Angiotension I. Then it tells the adrenal gland to produce Aldosterone. That process causes the body to hold onto water and sodium. All this is bad for the body. ACEI's block everyone of these pathways. There are medical studies showing how these medications decrease the blood pressure and the risk of death, protect the kidneys and decrease the risk of stroke and heart attacks. Common side effects from this type of antihypertensive include: hypotension (low blood pressure), hyperkalemia (high potassium which could lead to cardiac arrhythmias), angioedemia (swelling of lips and face) and a dry "tickle" cough.

<u>FAA Safe ACEI's</u>

1. **Accupril** (quinapril)

2. **Accuretic** (quinipril + hydrochlorthiazide {diuretic})

3. **Aceon** (perindopril)

4. **Altace** (ramipril)

5. **Capoten** (captopril)

6. **Lotensin (**benazepril)

7. **Mavik** (trandolapril)

8. **Monopril** (fosinopril)

9. **Prinivil and Zestril** (lisinopril)

10. **Prinizide** (lisinopril + hydrochlorthiazide)

11. **Univasc** - (moexipril)

12. **Vasotec** (enalapril)

Angiotensin Receptor Blockers (ARB) - This group of antihypertensive medications work in a similar way as **ACEI's**. **ARB's** work on the angiotensin receptor site instead of the multiple pathways explained above. This class of medication has very good clinical data and has been shown to decrease risk of death, stroke and can also protect the kidneys. Common side effects are: hypotension, hyperkalemia, angioedema and dry tickle cough. Angioedema and cough is much less than **ACEI's.**

FAA Safe ARB's

1. **Atacand** (candesartan)

2. **Avapro** (irbesartan)

3. **Azor** (olmesartan + amlodipine {vasodilator})

4. **Benicar** (olmesartan)

5. **Cozaar** (losartan)

6. **Diovan** (valsartan)

7. **Edarbyclor** (azilsartan)

8. **Exforge** (valsartan + amlodipine)

9. **Hyzaar** (losartan + hydrochlorthiazide)

10. **Micardis** (telmisartan)

Diuretics - This is a group of medications will eliminate from the body excess water, sodium, potassium, chloride and calcium. The body needs water for blood pressure. Excess sodium will also cause body's blood pressure to increase. Put excess water and sodium together in our bodies and the likelihood of hypertension will increase. The hypertension guidelines, that healthcare workers use as a guide suggest for essential hypertension, a reasonable first medication to start with will be a diuretic. Side effects of this group of medications would be: hypotension, hypokalemia (low potassium), hypocalcemia (low calcium) and hypochloremia (low chloride). Low potassium could lead to potentially fatal cardiac arrhythmias. A group of diuretics most commonly used are thaizide diuretics which work on a specific part of the kidney called the distal tubule.

FAA Safe Diuretics

1. **Diuril** - (chlorthiazide)

2. **Dyazide** - (hydrochlorthiazide + triamterene (potassium sparing diuretic)

3. **Dyrenium** - (triamterene)

4. **Hydrodiuril** - (hydrochlorthiazide)

5. **Maxide** - (hydrochlorthiazide + triamterine)

6. **Moduretic** - (hydrochlorthiazide + amiloride (potassium sparing diuretic)

7. **Mykrox** - (metolazone)

Beta Blockers - This is a group of medications that can be used in hypertension, heart failure and after a heart attack. As the name implies, a beta blocker blocks beta receptors. There are two different types of beta receptors, beta1 and beta2. The beta1 receptors are involved in increasing a persons heart rate. The beta2 receptors are in the lungs and will dilate the air sacs. I teach my students that the beta receptors reside in your **one** heart (Beta1 receptors) and **two** lungs (beta2 receptors). Beta blockers will decrease heart rate (block Beta1) and allow the bottom chambers of the heart to fill better. They will also decrease pressure in the heart and dilate the artery going out of the heart. This will help deliver more blood that is carrying oxygen to get delivered, like FEDEX to the brain, kidneys and peripheral organs and limbs. Side effects include: bradycardia (low heart rate), hypotension and heart block (a slowing of the electrical conduction system of the heart).

<u>FAA Safe Beta Blockers</u>

1. **Tenormin** - (atenolol)

2. **Bystolic** - (nebivolol)

3. **Cartrol** - (carteolol)

4. **Coreg** - (carvedilol)

5. **Corgard and Corzide** - (nadolol)

6. **Inderal** - (propranolol)

7. **Kerlone** - (betaxolol)

8. **Levatol** - (penbutalol)

9. **Lopressor and ToprolXL-** (metoprolol)

10. **Normodyne** - (labetalol)

11. **Sectral** - (acetbutolol)

12. **Visken** - (pindolol)

13. **Zebeta** - (bisoprolol)

14. **Ziac** - (bisoprolol + hydrochlorthiazide)

Calcium Channel Blockers - This group of medications have two categories. Calcium channels will allow calcium to go into the membranes and electrical channels of the heart to do their work. One group of calcium channel blockers (CCB) is called Dihydropyridines. This group of CCB's cause dilation of smooth muscle. The second group of calcium channel blockers, are called Non-dihydropyridines. This group are rate controllers. They will slow down the heart rate if the patient is going to fast (tachycardia). They work on two nodes located in the heart to decrease heart rate. Side effects include: bradycardia, hypotension, heart block, constipation and edema (accumulation of water in the legs).

FAA Safe Calcium Channel Blockers

1. **Adalat and Procardia** - (nifedipine)

2. **Calan and Covera** - (verapamil)

3. **Cardene** - (nicardipine)

4. **Cardizem and Tiazec**- (diltiazem)

5. **Lexxel and Plendil** - (felodipine)

6. **Lotrel** - (amlodipine + benazepril {ACEI})

7. **Norvasc** - (amlodipine)

8. **Procardia** - (nifedipine)

9. **Sular** - (nisoldipine)

Vasodilator - This group of medication dilates arterial smooth muscle (dilates the arteries). This means it dilates and relaxes the layers of the artery allowing more blood to pass through. Side effects: hypotension, dizziness, fast heart rate and headache.

1. **Apresoline** - (hydralazine)

Alpha Blockers - This is a group of medications that originally were used for Hypertension. They block a receptor that causes the vessels to vasoconstrict. When the vessels constrict, they get smaller and less blood gets through which causes the blood pressure to rise. This happens when we get in stressful situations. The body will produce substances like epinephrine, "Adrenaline," which will cause the alpha receptors to constrict and cause the blood pressure to rise. This is very similar to the Flight/Fright Response. You see something this is scary or not pleasant and you have two choices. Get tough and fight or get the heck out of Dodge. The body's reaction is to vasoconstrict and get that pressure up for your choice of fighting or fleeing. By blocking these receptors, with alpha blockers, blood pressure will lower. Side effects include: lightheadedness, drowsiness, tiredness and weight gain. The FAA lists the alpha blockers indications to decrease the symptoms of Benign Prostatic Hypertrophy (BPH) for all of us who have prostates.

FAA Safe Alpha Blockers for BPH

1. **Cardura** - (doxazosin)

2. **Flomax** - (terazocin)

3. **Minipress** - (prazosin)

Chapter 3
Diabetes Type I and II

Diabetes Mellitus is a disease where the pancreas is either producing inadequate amounts of insulin, poorly functional insulin or no insulin at all.

In Diabetes Type II patients, the amount of insulin produced by the pancreas is low and poorly function. Diabetes Type I patients, do not produce any insulin from the pancreas and exogenous insulin (injecting an insulin product) is needed to control very high glucose levels. Insulin regulates carbohydrate and fat metabolism. Insulin causes the liver, skeletal muscles and fat tissue to absorb glucose. Patients who have Pre-Diabetes, have no symptoms of diabetes, but have higher than normal Fasting Blood Glucose(FBG) levels. Normal FBG is < 100 mg/dL. If the FBG is ≥ 100 mg/dL and < 126 mg/dL, the patient is considered "prediabetic".

Patients who are diagnosed with prediabetes, almost always will become Type II Diabetics. This patient type can control their glucose levels with diet and exercise. Even Type II diabetes, with blood sugars close to 126 mg/dL are given a trial of diet and exercise. When diet and exercise cannot control the blood glucose levels, in patients with Diabetes Type II, medications are needed. Another blood test that is done is a Hemoglobin A1C. This test is a measure on how "sweet" the patient is over the last 2-3 months. A normal

HgA1C is 4- 5.6 %. Prediabetics will have HgA1C levels of 5.7% - 6.4%.

Diabetes Type II patients can get a 1st, 2nd and 3rd Class Medical Certificates. A Special Issuance is needed first. Diabetes Type I patients can only get a Third Class Medical Certificate.

There are a few different classes of Diabetes Type II medications. There are the sulfonylureas (**Glucotrol®**) which are "squeezers." The work by squeezing out the lower amounts of insulin or poorer quality insulin that reside in the pancreas. The glitazones (**Actose®**) work by stimulating the pancreas to produce insulin. Glitazones control the glucose and lipids in the muscle, fat tissue and liver. Alpha glucosidase (**Precose®**) inhibitors slow the breakdown of carbohydrates when they reach the stomach, thereby decrease the glucose spikes in the blood after a meal. Biguanides (**Glucophage®**) will suppress glucose production in the liver to help prevent hyperglycemia (high glucose levels). DDP-4 inhibitors (**Januvia®**) increase the release of insulin and suppress the release of glucagon which gets broken down into glucose. Incretin Mimetics (**Byetta®**) are a synthetic version of a hormone in your body called Incretin. Incretin tells the pancreas to release insulin after a meal. The primary side effect with all of the medications is hypoglycemia, except **Glucophage®** (metformin), which does not cause hypoglycemia.

Medications that increase insulin levels, like the sulfonylureas will also cause some weight gain. Metformin has a black box warning concerning lactic acidosis, which occurs very rarely. Meglitinides cause an increase in secretion of insulin from the pancreas.

There are many different Insulin products, used in Diabetes Type I that are very long acting, medium acting and short acting. The endocrinologist will personalize the kinds and doses of insulin based on the diabetic's blood sugar throughout the day.

The FAA is very specific in the criteria to keep and hold a 3rd Class Medical with Diabetes Type I.

Initial Certification

1. The applicant must have had no recurrent (two or more) episodes of hypoglycemia in the past 5 years and none in the preceding 1 year resulting in loss of consciousness, seizure, impaired cognitive function or requiring

intervention by another party, or occurring without warning (hypoglycemia unawareness).

2. The applicant will be required to provide copies of all medical records as well as accident and incident records pertinent to their history of diabetes.

3. A report of a complete medical examination preferably by a physician who specializes in the treatment of diabetes will be required. The report must include, as a minimum:

   ◦ Two measurements of glycated hemoglobin (total A1 or A1c concentration and the laboratory reference range), the first at least 90 days prior to the current measurement.

   ◦ Specific reference to the applicant's insulin dosages and diet.

   ◦ Specific reference to the presence or absence of cerebrovascular, cardiovascular, or peripheral vascular disease or neuropathy.

   ◦ Confirmation by an eye specialist of the absence of clinically significant eye disease.

   ◦ Verification that the applicant has been educated in diabetes and its control and understands the actions that should be taken if complications, especially hypoglycemia, should arise. The examining physician must also verify that the applicant has the ability and willingness to properly monitor and manage his or her diabetes.

○   If the applicant is age 40 or older, a report, with ECG tracings, of a maximal graded exercise stress test.

○   The applicant shall submit a statement from his/her treating physician, aviation medical examiner, or other knowledgeable person attesting to the applicants dexterity and ability to determine blood glucose levels using a recording glucometer).

The American Diabetic Association and the FAA have also published very specific criteria for pilots before, during and after landing.

IV. Glucose Management Prior to Flight, During Flight, and Prior to Landing

A. Individuals with ITDM shall maintain appropriate medical supplies for glucose management at all times while preparing for flight and while acting as pilot-in-command (or other flightcrew member). At a minimum, such supplies shall include:

1. An FAA-acceptable whole blood digital glucose monitor with memory;

2. Supplies needed to obtain adequate blood samples and to measure whole blood glucose; and

3. An amount of rapidly absorbable glucose, in 10 gram (gm) portions, appropriate to the potential duration of the flight.

B. All disposable supplies listed above must be within their expiration dates.

C. The individual with ITDM, acting as pilot-in-command or other flightcrew member, shall establish and document a blood glucose concentration equal to or greater than 100 milligrams/deciliter (mg/dl) but not greater than 300 mg/dl within 1/2 hour prior to takeoff. During flight, the individual with ITDM shall monitor his or her blood glucose concentration at hourly intervals and within 1/2 hour prior to landing. If a blood glucose concentration range of 100-300 mg/dl in not maintained, the following action shall be taken:

1. Prior to flight. The individual with ITDM shall test and record his or her blood glucose concentration within 1/2 hour prior to takeoff. If blood glucose measures less than 100 mg/dl, the individual shall ingest an appropriate 10 gm glucose snack (minimum 10 gm) and recheck and document blood glucose concentration after 1/2 hour. This process shall be repeated until blood glucose concentration is in the 100-300 mg/dl range. If

blood glucose concentration measures greater than 300 mg/dl, the individual shall follow his or her regimen of blood glucose control, as provided to the FAA by his or her attending physician, until the measurement of blood glucose concentration permits adherence to this protocol.

2. During flight.

(a) One hour into the flight, at each successive hour of flight, and within 1/2 hour prior to landing, the individual shall measure and document his or her blood glucose concentration. Listed below are blood glucose concentration ranges and the actions to be taken when they occur during flight:

(1) Less than 100 mg/dl: The individual shall ingest a 20 gm glucose snack and recheck and document his or her blood glucose concentration after 1 hour.

(2) 100-300 mg/dl: The individual may continue his or her flight as planned.

(3) Greater than 300 mg/dl: The individual shall land as soon as practicable at the nearest suitable airport.

(b) The individual, as pilot, is responsible for the safety of the flight and must remain cognizant of those factors that are important in its successful completion. Accordingly, in recognition of such elements as adverse weather, turbulence, air traffic control changes, or other variables, the individual may decide that a scheduled, hourly measurement of blood glucose concentration during the flight is of lower priority than the need for full, undivided attention to piloting. In such cases, the individual shall ingest a 10 gm glucose snack. One hour after ingesting of this glucose snack, the individual shall measure and document his or her blood glucose concentration. If the individual is unable to perform the measurement of his or her blood glucose concentration for the second consecutive time, the individual shall ingest a 20 gm glucose snack and shall land as soon as practicable at the nearest suitable airport. The individual, under these circumstances, is not required to measure and document his or her blood glucose concentration within 1/2 hour prior to landing.

3. Prior to landing. Except as noted above, the individual must measure and document his or her blood glucose concentration within 1/2 hour prior to landing.

FAA Guidelines for Diabetes Mellitus Type II controlled with Medications

PHARMACEUTICAL CONSIDERATIONS

Combination of DM medications with antihypertensives:

- Disqualifying Combinations. Certification of airmen using meglitinides or sulfonylureas, along with beta-blockers is not permitted. Commonly used meglitinides include repaglinide (Prandin) and nateglinide (Starlix). Commonly used sulfonylureas include: acetohexamide (Dymelor); chloropropamide (Diabinese); tolazamide (Tolinase); tolbutamide (Orinase); glimepiride (Amaryl); glipizide (Glucotrol,

Glucotrol XL); glyburide (DiaBeta, Micronase, Glynase); glyburide plus metformin (Glucovance); glipizide plus metformin (Metaglip).

- Allowable Combinations. Certification of airmen using the combination of a beta-blocker with the following diabetes medications is permitted: alpha-glucosidase inhibitors [acarbose (Precose), miglitol (Glyset)]; biguanides [metformin (Glucophage)]; thiazolidinediones [pioglitazone (Actos)]; DDP-4 inhibitors [sitagliptin (Januvia)]; and incretin mimetics [exenatide (Byetta)].

FAA Guidelines for Diabetes Mellitus Type I Medications

PHARMACEUTICAL CONSIDERATIONS

• Insulin pumps are an acceptable form of treatment.

• Combination of insulin with beta-bockers is not permitted

Combination of insulin with other anti-diabetes medication(s): not all combinations of DM medications are allowed by the FAA, even if each medication within the combination is acceptable as monotherapy. Contact Regional Flight Surgeon's office or AMCD.

Combination of insulin with other anti-diabetes medication (s): not all combinations of DM medications are allowed by the FAA, even if each medication within the combination is acceptable as monotherapy.

FAA Safe Medications for Diabetes Type II

1. **Actos** - (pioglitazone)

2. **Amaryl -** (glimepiride)

3. **Avandamet -** (rosiglitazone + metformin)

4. **Avandaryl -** (rosiglitazone + glimepiride)

5. **Avandia -** (rosiglitazone)

6. **Byetta -** (exenatide injection)

7. **Diabeta and Glynase -** (glyburide)

8. **Glucophage and Glumetza XR** - (metformin)

9. **Glucotrol -** (glipizide)

10. **Humulin, Novolin and Novolog-** (insulin)

11. **Janumet -** (sitagliptin + metformin)

12. **Januvia -** (stiagliptin)

13. **Kombiglize XR -** (saxagliptin + metformin)

14. **Lantus -** (insulin glargine)

15. **Levemir -** (insulin)

16. **Onglyza -** (saxagliptin)

17. **Precose -** (acarbose)

18. **Victoza -** (liraglutide {injection that is not like insulin})

Addressing the Disqualifying Combinations

The combination of Beta Blockers mixed with sulfonylureas or metiglitinides could potentially cause hyperglycemia. Beta Blockers can decrease the production of insulin which in turn will increase glucose levels. Beta Blockers also mask the symptoms of tremors and palpitations seen in hypoglycemia.

This interaction is not seen in alpha-glucosidase inhibitors {acarbose (Precose)}, {miglitol (Glyset)}, biguanides; metformin (Glucophage); thiazolidinediones {pioglitazone (Actos)}; DDP-4 inhibitors {sitagliptin (Januvia)}; and incretin mimetics {exenatide (Byetta)}.

Chapter 4
The Heart

Coronary Artery Disease

This is an area that is near and dear to my heart. Pun is intended. My area of expertise is evidence based, American College of Cardiology/American Heart Association Guidelines and cardiac medications that have been studied and proven to decrease death and a future risk of cardiac disease.

My primary gig is being a Clinical Pharmacist in the Cardiology arena. Coronary Artery disease includes Unstable Angina and two kinds of heart attacks. The symptoms of chest pain, that is not related to exercise or any other musculoskeletal disease is due to blood flow that is being blocked by a clot in the coronary arteries. Why the chest pain? Blood carries oxygen and when the oxygen cannot get delivered to the heart muscle, chest pain occurs. The chest pain will feel like an elephant sitting on the chest, a balloon blowing up in the chest and sometimes pain will radiate up the jaw and down the arm. A patient will start to grab their chest with a clenched fist, to the crushing chest pain. This is known as the Levine's Sign.

The physiology of the blockage is a decrease in blood flow due to the plaque. Not the stuff that accumulates on your teeth. I wish it would be that easy to grab some coronary paste, put it on a long, thin brush and scrub it away. The coronary arteries sit on top of the heart and supply blood to the heart muscle. Any extra cholesterol that is not being used by the body will find its way to the coronary arteries. The plaques are filled with cholesterol. An inflammatory process causes the plaques to rupture and clots are formed over the plaque in the coronary artery. I call them my angry platelets. I have given them a name. Their name is Al the Angry Platelet or Alice the Angry Platelet based on your gender. If the patient has crushing chest, EKG changes and a particular lab test elevation (Troponin), a procedure must be done to relieve the pain.

Unstable Angina is chest pain with no EKG changes and lab elevation. The patient is treated with medications. Heart attacks come in two varieties, Non-ST Elevation Myocardial Infarction (NSTEMI) and ST Elevation Myocardial Infarction (STEMI). NSTEMI's are heart attacks where the occlusion in the coronary artery is not total. STEMI are heart attacks where there is a complete occlusion of one of the coronary arteries.

Treatments for the heart attacks are coronary artery bypass surgery, percutaneous catheterization intervention (PCI) or balloon angioplasty. PCI is the most common intervention where a wire is put through the clot, a balloon is inserted to push the clot to the side walls and a stent is placed over a balloon and inserted into the coronary artery. When the balloon is deflated the stent will keep that coronary artery open and blood will flow to the heart muscle.

The patient will be told to exercise, eat healthy, control cholesterol, stop smoking and will be put on medications.

FAA and Coronary Artery Disease

The Federal Aviation Regulations (14 CFR 67) identify significant CAD, angina pectoris, and a history of myocardial infarction as disqualifying medical conditions. Part 67.401 states that, in order to obtain a special medical certificate, any applicant with one or more of these conditions must prove "to the satisfaction of the Federal Air Surgeon that the duties authorized by the class of medical certificate applied for can be performed without endangering public safety." What this really means is that if you have one of these conditions, then there is extra testing that you must do to show that you are still safe to operate aircraft. The following paragraphs outlines what is needed.

The following is required for **Class III** (recreational and private pilot duty) applicants:

1. Hospital admission summary (history and physical), coronary catheterization report, operative report and discharge summary regarding your infarction, angina, bypass surgery or angioplasty.

2. A current cardiovascular evaluation. This evaluation must include an assessment of personal and family medical history, a clinical cardiac examination and general physical examination, an assessment and statement regarding the applicant's medications, functional capacity, modifiable cardiovascular risk factors, motivation for any necessary change and prognosis for incapacitation during the certification period; and a current report of fasting blood sugar and a blood lipid profile to

include: total cholesterol, HDL, LDL and triglycerides.

3.   A maximal ECG treadmill stress test must be performed no sooner than 6-months post event. All stress testing should achieve 100 percent of maximal predicted heart rate unless medically contraindicated or prevented either by symptoms, conditioning, or concurrent use of medication; such as, B-blockers, calcium channel blockers (spec. diltiazem and verapamil), and/or digitalis preparations. With the consent of the attending physician, these medications should be discontinued for at least 48 hours prior to testing in order to attain maximal stress.

The following is required for **Class I** and **Class II** applicants:

1.   First- and second-class certificates may be issued only by AAM-300 and only upon the recommendation of one or more of the Federal Air Surgeon's consultants, providing the requirements of paragraphs 1, 2 and 3 from above (for class III) are met. Six-month post event coronary angiography is required, and dynamic radionuclide

myocardial perfusion must reveal no evidence of ischemia
or significant myocardial dysfunction.

2.	Consideration for the issuance of a functionally limited
second-class certificate (e.g., "Not Valid for
Carrying Passengers or Cargo for
Compensation or Hire", etc.) is reserved for
AAM-300. Requests for consideration must be
accompanied by a completed Operational
Questionnaire (FAA Form 8500-20).

Before certification can be considered, a six-month recovery
period must elapse. If the applicant has had a heart attack, then this
allows time for the heart to adequately heal. If the individual has
undergone a procedure, the most likely time that a restenosis
(renarrowing) will occur is during the first six months. After this
time, complications are much less likely.

The FAA will consider an Authorization for a Special Issuance of a
Medical Certificate (Authorization) for most cardiac conditions.
Applicants seeking further FAA consideration should be prepared
to submit all past records and a report of a complete current
cardiovascular evaluation in accordance with FAA specifications.

Medications in Coronary Artery Disease

The medication regimen used in coronary artery disease post-intervention is two antiplatelet medications, an anti-ischemic medications and a cholesterol medication.

The first antiplatelet medication is aspirin. Aspirin will decrease the chance for another heart attack by 20%. It also will help keep the stent open. Aspirin will be combined with another antiplatelet medication called an ADP receptor inhibitor. ADP receptor inhibitors work in synergy with the aspirin to keep the stent open and decrease the risk of death and future heart attacks. Examples of ADP receptor inhibitors are **Ticlid** (ticlopidine), **Plavix®** (clopidogrel)**, Effient®** (prasugrel), and **Brilinta®** (ticagrelor). The biggest side effect of aspirin and ADP receptor blockers is bleeding. The most common bleeding reported is gastrointestinal bleeding and ulcers. GI medications such as **Pepcid®** (famotidine) and **Prilosec®** (omeprazole) are commonly prescribed to prevent GI bleeding.

The anticholesterol medications play a huge role in preventing future heart attacks and coronary artery disease. This category of anti-cholesterol medications are called, "Statins." This group of medications decrease the production of cholesterol and are very important to take on a daily basis. The physician will take a Lipid

Panel which includes the measure of LDL (low density lipid "bad cholesterol"), HDL (high density lipid "good cholesterol") and triglycerides. The statins will decrease LDL, increase HDL (about 6%) and decrease triglycerides. Examples of statins are **Mevacor®** (lovastatin), **Pravachol®** (pravastatin), **Lescol®** (fluvastatin), **Lipitor®** (atorvastatin), **Zocor®** (simvastatin), **Livalo®** (pitavastatin) and **Crestor®** (rosuvastin). The most common side effects from statins are muscle aches and possible liver failure.

Niacin is another anticholesterol medications that has been used in addition to statins. Niacin has not been studied as extensively as the Statin medications. Niacin is added to the regimen when the statins are not decreasing the LDL and triglycerides to the degree wanted by the physician. This is another of the "It does everything, but keep your Mother-In-Law away" anticholesterol medications. Niacin decreases LDL, triglycerides and increases HDL. It is one of the best medications to increase the "good cholesterol" HDL. The HDL molecules are the "hunters and gatherers." HDL will grab the cholesterol sitting in the coronary arteries and take the cholesterol back to the liver and get broken down. The long acting Niacin products seem to work the best and have the least amount of side effects. An example of a long acting Niacin is **Niaspan®** (niacin extended release). The biggest side effect seen with niacin is flushing. The antidote for the flushing is aspirin. I counsel patients, in the hospital on their cardiac medications. I recommend the patients on Niacin, who are always on aspirin, to take their long acting niacin with their prescribed aspirin.

Fibrates are another class of anticholesterol medications that are prescribed with statins, when the statins are not decreasing the triglycerides and LDL to the degree anticipated by the cardiologist. Fibrates are prescribed when the triglyceride levels are not decreasing. Examples of fibrates are, **Lopid®** (gemfibrozil) and **Tricor®** (fenofibrate). The biggest side effects are GI upset and muscle pain. There also is a possible drug interaction with statins that could cause an increase in muscle pain, that is not musculoskeletal in nature.

Bile Acid Sequesterants are another class of anticholesterol medications. This medication is a resin and will bind with the bile acids in the intestine and get excreted in the feces. Plasma cholesterol will be converted to bile acids to replenish the bile acid loss and cholesterol levels will decrease. It usually comes in a packet and you mix it with water. It tastes like sand and if it is orange flavored tastes like orange sand. Compliance is an issue. Side effects are constipation, increased triglycerides and gallstones. This product is not used much anymore due to the above side effects. Example of a bile acid sequestrant is **Questran®**

(cholesteramine) and **Welchol®** (colesevelam). **Welchol®** is a tablet taken one to two times a day. It is much better tolerated than **Questran®**.

Their are two medications that are placed in their own class of anticholesterol medications. **Zetia®** (ezetimibe) decreases the absorption of cholesterol in the intestine. Ezetimibe is usually used in combination with simvastatin. A brand new combination is with Atorvastatin and Ezetimibe. The Omega 3 fatty acids have been used as an adjunct to statin therapy. They are found naturally in fish, especially, salmon, tuna and mackerel. Omego 3 Fatty acids will decrease triglycerides and blood pressure. An example of Omega 3 fatty acids is **Lovaza®** (omega 3 fatty acid).

Beta Blockers will also be part of the cardiac medications post heart attack and unstable angina. Beta Blockers are anti-ischemic medications and help the heart get stronger and deliver more oxygen to the organs (See Hypertension medications for the listing of Beta Blockers). The Beta Blocker medication that has the best evidence is **Coreg®** (carvedilol). This is my "Blueberry Beta Blocker". It has antioxidant effects, increases insulin sensitivity, strengthens the heart and decreases mortality. As a review, side effects will include, bradycardia (low heart rate) and hypotension (low blood pressure).

Angiotensin Converting Enzyme Inhibitors (ACEI) will be added to the coronary artery disease regimen. They are especially important if the patient has a poor pumping heart and are a diabetic. ACEI's strengthen the heart and protect the diabetic kidney. ACEI will also decrease the remodeling of the heart after a heart attack. I am not talking about remodeling your house or kitchen. The heart, when weakened and injured will get bigger to try and pump better. It will also get fibrotic (stiff). A stiff heart does not pump and fill well. ACEI's will reverse this remodeling. Side effects include, hyperkalemia (high potassium), change in renal function, hypotension, angioedema and a dry tickle cough (See Hypertension medications for the listing of ACEI's).

Angiotensin Receptor Blockers (ARB) will be added instead of an ACEI is some cases. This is usually seen when the patient cannot tolerate an ACEI. The cough becomes too much of a quality of life issue and will be switched to an ARB (See Hypertension medications for the listing of ARB's).

FAA Safe Medications for Coronary Heart Disease

1. **Aspirin** (aspirin) - antiplatelet

2. **Crestor®** (rosuvastatin) - anticholesterol

3. **Effient®** (prasugrel) - antiplatelet

4. **Lescol®** (fluvastatin) - anticholesterol

5. **Lipitor®** (atorvastatin) - anticholesterol

6. **Livalo®** (pitavastatin) - anticholesterol

7. **Lopid®** (gemfibrozil) - anticholesterol

8. **Lovaza®** (omega 3 fatty acid) - anticholesterol

9. **Mevacor®** (lovastatin) - anticholesterol

10. **Niaspan®** (niacin extended release) - anticholesterol

11. **Omacor®** (omega 3 fatty acid) - anticholesterol

12. **Plavix®** (clopidogrel) - antiplatelet

13. **Pravachol®** (pravastatin) - anticholesterol

14. **Questran®** (cholesteramine) - anticholesterol

15. **Ticlid®** (ticlopidine) - antiplatelet

16. **Tricor® , Triglide® and Trilipix®** (fenofibrate) - anticholesterol

17. **Welchol®** (colesevelam)

18. **Vytorin®** (simvastatin + ezetimibe)

Cardiac Arrhthmias

The most common cardiac arrhythmia seen in the patient population is atrial fibrillation. You will hear and see atrial fibrillation mentioned on the internet and television as "Afib." The heart has four chambers with a type of electrical circuitry throughout the heart muscle. The top chamber, left and right is called the atrium. The bottom chamber, left and right is called the ventricle. We have a sinus node in the atria that controls the heart rate. We have a node called the AV (atrioventricular) node that connects the circuitry from the atria to the ventricles. The AV node sits between the bottom of the atrium and the top of the ventricle. The beat goes through AV node into a path called the His-Purkinje fibers that carry the beats to the ventricle for that chamber to contract. If the heart rate is too high, the blood will not fill the ventricle very well and the blood will not be pumped to the brain, kidneys and organs in an efficient manner. Any reason, such as Asthma, Chronic Obstructive Pulmonary Disease (COPD), other pulmonary disease will stretch the atrium. The stretch will cause the atrial pacemakers to all go off at once. They are going really, really fast. The rates seen is around 300 beats per minute. The AV node will only let about 150 of these beats per minute go through to the ventricle. The heart is going very fast and irregular. There is a possibility of a clot being formed in the atria due to the turbulence caused by the fast rate. If these clots get shot out to the brain, a stroke will happen.

So how does the physicians treat atrial fibrillation? They will use antiarrhythmic medications to convert the patient to a normal sinus rhythm. People with atrial fibrillation can also be treated with medications to control the heart rate. These patients on rate control and antiarrhythmic control will also be placed on anticoagulants to prevent clots being formed. Atrial fibrillation can be chronic or paroxysmal (stops and starts).

Medications prescribed in Atrial Fibrillation

The antiarrhythmic medications are "bad rhythm" converters. They are designed to convert the bad rhythm to the good rhythm. I call them "chemical cardioverters." The medications is this category include: **Cordarone®, Mexitil®, Multaq®, Norpace®, Rythmol®** and **Tambocor®.** The unique side effect of all of them are cardiac arrhythmias. I am sure you are chuckling at this. How can an antiarrhythmic cause an arrhythmia? They work on channels in the heart and change how the beats are transmitted. If it slows too much the beat will look like a guinea pig exercising in the round spinning cage. **Cordarone®** is an unique antiarrhthmic in that it will control the rate of the heart and convert the bad rhythm. **Cordarone®** has four unique side effects. It can cause pulmonary fibrosis, hypo/hyperthyroidism, lenticular opacities (yellow floaties in the eyes) and blue/grey skin discoloration (Smurf nose,cheeks and ears). **Cordarone®** is the most used and safest of the antiarrhythmics used in people with atrial fibrillation. **Multaq®** works in a very similar manner as **Cordarone®**, but with less side effects. **Multaq®** is contraindicated in patients with

75

bad heart failure. **Tambocor®** side effects include: dizziness, vision problems, shortness of breath, headache, nausea, shaking, tiredness, or weakness. **Mexitil®** side effects include: dizziness, heartburn, nausea, nervousness, trembling and unsteadiness. **Rythmol®** side effects are dizziness, headache, metallic/salty taste in the mouth, nausea/vomiting, constipation, anxiety, and tiredness. Another group of medications used in atrial fibrillation are the rate controllers. Controlling the fast heart rate of atrial fibrillation is imperative if the patient is not going to be on an antiarrhythmic. The heart rate on these medications should be between 60 and 100 beats per minute. The patient with afib should be, not too fast and not too slow. Sorry for the Three Little Bears analogy. The rate control medications include: **Calan®**, **Cardizem CD®**, **Coreg®**, **Lopressor®**, **Toprol XL®** and **Tenormin®**. Side effects seen with all these medications include: bradycardia (low heart rate), hypotension, drowsiness, dizziness, syncope (fainting) and heart block.

The anticoagulant medications are used in atrial fibrillation to prevent clots, strokes in particular. The side effects are bleeding. Gastrointestinal and brain bleeds being the most common.

The most common anticoagulant used is **Coumadin®** (warfarin). Warfarin has a incredible story on how we came about taking warfarin. It has been known as "rat poison." Warfarin evolved as a medication due to a drought in the early 1920's. Sweet clover had to be used as feed for cattle and every now and then it would get moldy. When the cattle ate it they would bleed. The cattle people (I am very PC) would take their cattle to the vet and would have to be transfused. Once in a while, the cattle would die from bleeding and upon autopsy found in their belly or bellies, bishydroxycoumarin. They said, " we cannot give this to people, so let's kill rats with this stuff." The farmers would sprinkle warfarin in corn meal. The rats would eat it, bump up against something and would bleed to death. In the mid 50's, the American Heart Association said let us study this. So follow along with me, The **W**isconsin **A**lumni **R**esearch **F**oundation took coum**arin** (**WARFARIN**) and that is how warfarin got it's name. In the beginning warfarin was used for heart attacks and the first celebrity to get warfarin was Dwight David Eisenhower, former president of the United States, for his heart attack. At a later time the medical field used warfarin for deep vein thrombosis (DVT), Atrial fibrillation and Pulmonary Embolism. When taking warfarin, the patient must have labs drawn on a regular basis to see if they are therapeutic. There are many drug interactions (> 600 reported) that could cause an increase risk of bleeding. It is a bit of work to ensure the warfarin is doing its job.

In November of 2011, a novel oral anticoagulant was approved for stroke prevention in atrial fibrillation called **Xarelto®**. It is taken once a day. It has very few drug interactions and there is no lab monitoring required. The primary side is bleeding and less brain bleeds than warfarin. This was followed by another anticoagulant called **Eliquis®** (apixaban) to prevent stroke in atrial fibrillation. Apixaban, also has very few drug interactions and does not need to be monitored. It also could cause major bleeding.

FAA

The applicant with chronic or paroxysmal atrial fibrillation will require and **Initial Special Issuance.** This will require an FAA decision. A follow up special issuance is also required. A history of resolved atrial fibrillation of greater than 5 years, with no ischemia (inability to perfuse organs), history of clot, structural or functional will be issued a medical certificate. Otherwise a FAA decision will be required.

FAA Safe Medications

1. **Calan®** - (verapamil) rate controller
2. **Cardizem®** - (diltiazem) rate controller
3. **Cordarone® and Pacerone®** - (amiodarone) antiarrhythmic
4. **Coreg®** - (carvedilol) rate controller
5. **Coumadin®** - (warfarin) anticoagulant
6. **Eliquis®** - (apixaban) anticoagulant

7. **Lopressor® and Toprol®**- (metoprolol tartrate) rate controller

8. **Mexitil®** - (mexilitene) antiarrhythmic

9. **Multaq®** - (dronedarone) antiarrhythmic

10. **Norpace®** - (disopyramide) antiarrhythmic

11. **Rythmol®** - (propafenone) antiarrhythmic

12. **Tambocor®** - (flecainide) antiarrhythmic

13. **Tenormin®** - (atenolol) rate controller

14. **Tiazec®** - (diltiazem) rate controller

15. **Xarelto®** - (rivaroxaban) anticoagulant

Chapter 5
Deep Vein Thrombosis (DVT)
Pulmonary Embolism (PE)

Clots can form just about anywhere in the body. When clots form and occlude a vein in the leg, it is called a deep vein thrombosis (DVT). In most cases, a DVT is formed in people who are obese, lung disease and are bed ridden. In some people clots form spontaneously due to blood problems. This patient population are hypercoagulable. This means they are clot factories. DVT's are very painful and need to be anticoagulated. Lay people will call this, "thinning the blood."
Clots can move from the legs to the lungs. The clots will clog up the pulmonary vessels. This is
a very serious condition and could lead to bad consequences. The patient will be unable to breath and needs to get to a hospital.

The medications that are used in DVT and PE are anticoagulants. The patients will go home on an anticoagulant for three, six, nine or twelve months. If **Coumadin® is** prescribed for DVT or PE, lab tests to ensure a therapeutic level will be drawn on a regular basis. See the atrial fibrillation section for anticoagulants for warfarin information. A new anticoagulant, **Xarelto®** has come on the market that requires no lab monitoring. As before its main side effect is abnormal bleeding. People with DVT or PE may also go home on a Heparin-like injection called Lovenox®. This injection can be used by itself or as a bridge to **Coumadin®**. The side effect of **Lovenox®** is bleeding. It is usually injected twice a day. These are the same anticoagulants that are used in atrial fibrillation.

FAA for DVT, PE, and Coagulopathies

AASI FOR DEEP VENOUS THROMBOSIS (DVT), PULMONARY EMBOLISM (PE), AND/ OR HYPERCOAGULOPATHIES

AME Assisted Special Issuance (AASI) is a process that provides Examiners the ability to re-issue an airman medical certificate under the provisions of an Authorization for Special Issuance of a Medical Certificate (Authorization) to an applicant who has a medical condition that is disqualifying under Title 14 of the Code of Federal Regulations (14 CFR) part 67.

An FAA physician provides the initial certification decision and grants the Authorization in accordance with 14 CFR § 67.401. The Authorization letter is accompanied by attachments that specify the information that treating physician(s) must provide for the re-issuance determination. If this is a first-time application for an AASI for the above disease/condition and the applicant has all the required medical information necessary for a determination, the Examiner must defer and submit all of the documentation to the AMCD or RFS for the initial determination.

Examiners may re-issue an airman medical certificate under the provisions of an Authorization, if the applicant provides the following:

- An Authorization granted by the FAA;

- A summary of the applicant's medical condition since the last FAA medical examination, including a statement regarding any further episodes of DVT,

PE or other complication of hypercoagulopathy (see below*);

- The name and dosage of medication(s) used for treatment and/or prevention with comment regarding side effects; and

- A minimum of monthly International Normalized Ratio (INR) results for the immediate prior 6 months for those being treated with warfarin (Coumadin).

* The Examiner must defer to the AMCD or Region if:

- More than 20 percent of INR values are <2.0 or >3.0 for those being treated with warfarin (Coumadin); or

- The applicant develops emboli, thrombosis, bleeding that required medical intervention, or any other cardiac or neurologic condition previously not diagnosed or reported.

FAA Safe Medications

1. **Coumadin®** - (warfarin)
2. **Lovenox®** - (enoxaparin) anticoagulant injection
3. **Xarelto®** - (rivaroxaban)

Chapter 6
Lung Asthma Chronic Obstructive Pulmonary Disease (COPD)

Asthma is an inflammatory disease of the lungs. Asthma, when diagnosed is treated with inhaled corticosteroids and rescue bronchodilator inhalers. The primary treatment in asthma is inhaled corticosteroid medications to prevent asthma and to decrease the triggers that cause the inflammation. Leukotriene blockers are also used in asthma to decrease inflammation caused by leukotrienes.

Leukotrienes in the body cause inflammation. COPD is a chronic pulmonary disease with very poor airflow in the lungs. Most people with chronic bronchitis have COPD. The most common cause of COPD is smoking. Pollutants and irritants also cause COPD. Emphysema plays a role in COPD. Inhaled bronchodilators, anticholinergics and corticosteroids are also mainstay medications used in COPD, Inhaled bronchodilators open up the lungs. Inhaled corticosteroids decrease inflammation. Inhaled anticholinergics relax and dilate the airways, protect from bronchial spasms and decrease the mucous produced by the airways. Antibiotics are sometimes an additive medication used in COPD.

The lungs have receptors that when stimulated cause bronchodilation (opening of the lung air sacs). In asthmatic patients, the lung sacs are inflamed and constricted.

Corticosteroids that are inhaled prevent and control the inflammation seen in asthmatic patients. These are not the steroids that body builders use. This is the perfect way to get steroids to the lungs. Examples of inhaled steroids are: **Advair®, Aerobid®, Qvar®,** and **Symbicort®** (corticosteroid + bronchodilator). Side effects include, cough and possible fungal infection of the mouth. It is a must that after these inhalers are used that the user washes out their mouth after each dose. In children, a side effect is a decrease in growth as corticosteroids decrease the bone growth. Oral corticosteroids can also be used, but this is not the best way to take steroids. **Prednisone** is the most common oral steroid used. The oral steroids have many more side effects than inhaled steroids. The oral steroid side effects include: moon face, retention of sodium and water, osteoporosis, GI bleeding, nausea, euphoria (in high doses), blood sugar abnormalities and cataracts. This list keeps going on and on.

Bronchodilators open up the bronchioles in the lungs. This is where inhaled Beta 2 agonists work to open up the airways and decrease spasm. In asthma, the beta 2 agonists can be used as a rescue inhaler. The person feels bronchospasm coming on quickly and a couple of puffs on the beta agonist inhaler will decrease spasm and open up the bronchioles quickly. Inhaled steroids could also be used before exercise to prevent spasm and facilitate better oxygen exchange and supply. The biggest side effect observed with inhaled beta 2 agonists is tachycardia (high heart rate) after inhalation. This effect will be self-limiting and go away after a few minutes. Other side effects include, nervousness, shakiness, headache, nausea and vomiting.

Two devices for folks with asthma that I highly recommend is spacers and Peak Flow Meters. The spacers make it easier to get the medicine into the lungs. The patient will press the canister that holds the inhaled medicine and the patient will inhale to get the good stuff into their lungs. Peak Flow Meters can be used to predict when an asthmatic attack may occur. The patient take a big breath in and blows through the tube. It will tell the patient how much force has been blown through the tube. The patient can see if low, that an attack may occur.

FAA and Asthma

AME Assisted Special Issuance (AASI) is a process that provides Examiners the ability to re-issue an airman medical certificate under the provisions of an Authorization for Special Issuance of a Medical Certificate (Authorization) to an applicant who has a medical condition that is disqualifying under Title 14 of the Code of Federal Regulations (14 CFR) part 67.

An FAA physician provides the initial certification decision and grants the Authorization in accordance with 14 CFR § 67.401. The Authorization letter is accompanied by attachments that specify the information that treating physician(s) must provide for the re-issuance determination. If this is a first-time application for an AASI for the above disease/condition, and the applicant has all the requisite medical information necessary for a determination, the Examiner must defer and submit all of the documentation to the AMCD or RFS for the initial determination.

Examiners may re-issue an airman medical certificate under the provisions of an Authorization, if the applicant provides the following:

- An Authorization granted by the FAA;

- The applicant's current medical status that addresses frequency of attacks and whether the attacks have resulted in emergency room visits or hospitalizations;

- The Examiner should caution the applicant to cease flying with any exacerbation as warned in § 61.53;

- The name and dosage of medication(s) used for treatment and/or prevention with comment regarding side effects; and

- Results of pulmonary function testing, if deemed necessary, performed within the last 90 days

The Examiner must defer to the AMCD or Region if:

- The symptoms worsen;

- There has been an increase in frequency of emergency room, hospital, or outpatient visits;

- The FEV1 is less than 70% predicted value;

- The applicant requires 3 or more medications for stabilization; or

- The applicant is taking steroid doses equivalent to more than 20 mg of prednisone per day.

FAA and COPD

AME Assisted Special Issuance (AASI) is a process that provides Examiners the ability to re-issue an airman medical certificate under the provisions of an Authorization for Special Issuance of a Medical Certificate (Authorization) to an applicant who has a medical condition that is disqualifying under Title 14 of the Code of Federal Regulations (14 CFR) part 67.

An FAA physician provides the initial certification decision and grants the Authorization in accordance with 14 CFR § 67.401. The Authorization letter is accompanied by attachments that specify the information that treating physician(s) must provide for the re-issuance determination. If this is a first-time application for an AASI for the above disease/condition, and the applicant has all the requisite medical information necessary for a determination, the Examiner must defer and submit all of the documentation to the AMCD or RFS for the initial determination.

Examiners may re-issue an airman medical certificate under the provisions of an Authorization, if the applicant provides the following:

- An Authorization granted by the FAA;

- A statement regarding symptomatology of the condition;

- A statement addressing any associated illnesses, such as heart failure;

- The name and dosage of medication(s) used for treatment and/or prevention with comment regarding side effects; and

- A pulmonary specialist evaluation that includes the results of a current pulmonary function test, performed within the last 90 days The Examiner must defer to the AMCD or Region if:

- The FEV1 or FEV1/FVC is less than 70%;

- The applicant has developed an associated cardiac condition, or

- The applicant is taking steroid doses equivalent to more than 20 mg of prednisone per day.

FAA Safe Medications

1. **Accolate®** - (zafirlukast) leukotriene modifier

2. **Advair®** - (fluticasone + sameterol) beta agonist and antiinflammatory

3. **Aerobid®** - (flunisolide) antiinflammatory

4. **Atrovent®** - (ipratropium) anticholinergic

5. **Combivent®** - (ipratropium + albuterol) anticholinergic and bronchodilator

6. **Flovent®** - (fluticasone) antiinflammatory

7. **Prednisone®** - (prednisone) oral corticosteroid

8. **Proventil®** - (albuterol) bronchodilator

9. **Qvar®** - (beclomethasone) antiinflammatory

10. **Serevent®** - (salmeterol) bronchodilator

11. **Spiriva®** - (tiotropium) anticholinergic

12. **Symbicort®** - (budesonide + formoterol) antinflammatory + bronchodilator

13. **Theodur® and Uniphyl®** - (theophylline) bronchodilator

14. **Xopenex®** - (levabuterol) bronchodilator

Chapter 7
OVER THE COUNTER (OTC) MEDICATIONS

The most important point to know about Over The Counter (OTC) medications is that at one time, these products could only be dispensed with a physician's prescription. They are still chemicals that, when used for the proper malady works to alleviate symptoms. The flip side is that they also have side effects, many of which affects our piloting the aircraft.

A new medication, after it has been tested and studied will have a seventeen year patent life. The medication can then be made generically by many other pharmaceutical companies after the patent has expired. The FDA will review some of the most widely used medications and if they feel the public can take this medication safely, deem it an OTC medication.

The pharmaceutical companies will produce the medication and package it and sell it over the counter. As you well know, half of the pharmacy floor space is taken up by some OTC medication. The early pharmacies used to be called apothecaries. The pharmacist would get a prescription that was a recipe of different chemicals, plants or a combination thereof. The pharmacist would take the prescription and grind, add liquids, prepare powders to be taken. The pharmacist had a recipe book for the prescriptions, kind of like a cook book. I remember when I had an upset stomach being given a product called Paragoric®. It came in a dropper bottle and I had a few drops put into my mouth and swallow. It had quite a kick. My mom bought it at the local drug store. When I was in pharmacy school, I learned what was in Paragoric®. It had tincture of Opium. Did Larry say opium, the stuff that comes from poppy? You bet I did. Opium was an OTC. I live right across the street from Canada and you could get a cough syrup call Terpin Hydrate with Codeine. I had also heard from a fellow pharmacist that another very popular product was Terpin Hydrate with Heroine. What?!

I will take the most common OTC products from the FAA Accepted Medications and explain what you need to know when taking and how they may affect your flight.

The most common OTC's are the antihistamines, GI (gastrointestinal) medications, cold preparations with antihistamines, cough suppressants, pain relievers, constipation relievers, anti-diarrhea, and sleep products. Very soon, one of the statins will be released for OTC use for cholesterol. Antihistamines are self explanatory. When a person has an allergic reaction to a substance inhaled or taken, the body produces histamines. There are four different histamine receptors. The two most important to pilots are H1 and H2 histamines. The H1 histamines are involved with bronchoconstriction in the lungs, hives, pain and itching and primarily the allergic symptoms of nasal congestion, sleep and motion sickness. The H2 histamines are involved in gastric secretion.

The most popular of the H1 antihistamines is **Benadryl®** (diphenhydramine). It is used OTC as a capsule, liquid and topical cream. We use it in the hospital in IV form for allergic reactions to medications. Diphenhydramine works very well. It is given four times a day for severe allergic reactions. It's side effect profile is very simple and significant. It causes drowsiness and not just a little, but a lot. People who take it at night will wakeup with what we call "hangover effect." The effects of one dose will last for at least twelve hour. Can you imagine flying an airplane into a busy airport and accepting a LAHSO on **Benadryl®**? Besides sedation, the person who takes diphenhydramine will have dry mouth. This will lead to taking in more fluids which will lead to many visits to the bathroom. I teach to hold a medication for four half lives to ensure full elimination from the body of the medication. This means usually, that if the medication is given every 4 hours (six times a day) to wait for 24 hours (4 x 6). The FAA take this rule a step further. They say multiple the times you take a medication per day by **five (5)**. So if given 4 times a day (4x5 = 20). **Benadyl®** is NOT approved by the FAA as safe to take. **Drixoral®** is a first generation antihistamine that was very popular and better than Benadryl®. The FAA has put a 24 hour wait after ingesting a dose before a flight can be taken. **Dramamine®** is a first generation antihistamine that is used for motion sickness. This is a passengers only medication that can be purchased OTC. For pilots. there is a permanent restriction from taking **Dramamine®**. Along came second generation H1 antihistamines that cause less sedation. The second generation antihistamines are called non-sedating antihistamines which include: **Allegra®, Claritin®** and **Zyrtec®**. These three antihistamines are now available OTC. The pilot must wait 48 hours after the last dose of **Zyrtec®** before flight. **Zyrtec®** is the most sedation of the non-sedating antihistamines. **Allegra®** and **Claritin®** can be taken before flight. They can cause sedation in certain people. The best way to evaluate if sedation will occur is to take the medication at night and see if you get sedation. I have done some research into the how the FAA has dealt with airline pilots when the non-sedating antihistamines hit the market. If the airline pilots put on their medical form that they were taking the above mentioned antihistamines and reported no side effects they could fly after taking the non-sedating antihistamines. There is only one decongestant, besides normal saline, that works and is called **Sudafed®**. It works well and drys the nasal passages. Side effects are hypertension, should not be given if there is a prostate problem, drowsiness and wakefulness. The other tidbit you need to know is that pseudoephedrine has been used as an ingredient in "Meth." When I go to get pseudoephedrine for my family, I have to give the pharmacy my drivers license and it goes into a state record. Makes you feel a little weird, but this product works.

FAA PHARMACEUTICAL CONSIDERATIONS: For Hay Fever Requiring Antihistamines:

- The nonsedating antihistamines loratadine, desloratadine, and fexofenadine may be used while flying if, **after an adequate initial "trial period,"** symptoms are controlled without adverse side effects.

- Applicants with seasonal allergies requiring any other antihistamine (oral and/or nasal) may be certified by the examiner **only as follows:**

  - **With the stipulation that they do not exercise the privileges of airman certificate while taking the medication, AND**

  - **Wait after the last dose until** either:

At least five maximal dosing intervals*have passed. For example,if the medication is taken every 4-6 hours, wait 30 hours (5x6) after the last dose to fly, or,

At least five times the maximum terminal elimination half-life has passed. For example, if the medication half-life* is 6-8 hours, wait 40 hours (5x8) after the last dose to fly.

* Examiners are encouraged to look up the dosing intervals and half-life.

- For hay fever controlled by Desensitization, AME must warn airman to not operate aircraft until four hours after each injection.

- Airmen who are exhibiting symptoms, regardless of the treatment used, must not fly.

If the pilot is taking allergy shots, they must wait four hours after each injection before flying.

H2 receptor antihistamines are GI medications. The indications for these group of medications is gastroesophageal reflux disease (GERD), dyspepsia (heart burn) and stomach ulcers. The medications included in this group are **Tagamet®, Zantac®,** and **Pepcid®**. These medications block the action of histamine in the parietal cells that produce hydrochloric acid. Very few side effects have been seen but some include: dizziness, constipation, diarrhea and confusion. The majority of these sides effects are seen with **Tagamet®**. Overall they are very well tolerated.

Since we have been speaking about GI OTC's, we need to address Proton Pump Inhibitors(PPI). The medications included in this group is: **Prilosec®** (omeprazole) and **Prevacid®** (lansoprazole). There is also a combination product called **Zegerid®** (omeprezole plus sodium bicarbonate) which is a PPI and antacid product. These medications completely block the pumps that secrete hydrochloric acid. Side effects seen, though few are headache, nausea, diarrhea, abdominal pain, fatigue and dizziness. There has been some data saying patients who take PPI's have an increased risk of food allergies. There is no data as of yet is if this happen with long term and short term use. This has also been mentioned in people taking H2 receptor antihistamines as well. There has also been reported in the medical literature increased cases of patients taking PPI's that develop a severe form of diarrhea called Clostridium difficile (C diff). Please report multiple visits to the bathroom due to diarrhea, to your physician if you are taking PPI's. This is probably due to the PPI changed the environment of the gut to a different pH (acid to base) and allowing certain bacteria to flourish.

Nonsteroidal Antiinflammatory Drugs (NSAID)

Aspirin is one of the first NSAID's used for pain relief that was not an opioid. It is a derivative of white willow bark. Bayer was the first company to take aspirin powder and make it into a tablet. Bayer was also the first company to make chewable aspirin. I had an idea for better treatment in the Emergency Department for chewable aspirin. As mentioned in a previous chapter, aspirin is the first medication given for patients with heart attacks. If a patient can chew four baby aspirin it will be absorbed under the tongue and in the gut. If Dr. Hoffman had not come up with this formulation, it would be tougher to get aspirin on board quickly in our heart attack patients. My idea was to dress up as a PEZ dispenser and ***dispense*** four baby aspirin to everyone having chest pain. The orange flavor of course would be the only choice. I would like to reiterate that 325 mg of aspirin is NOT four times as potent as 81 mg (baby aspirin). The higher dose causes more GI bleeding and hemorrhage in the brain. The indications for aspirin is for heart attacks (MI's) after catheterization, for stroke prevention, for stroke treatment and for stroke prevention in atrial fibrillation. I have heard many big time cardiologists say that if aspirin was a new drug going to the FDA (not the FAA), it would not be allowed on the market due to the side effects.

The two most popular NSAIDS, over the counter are **Motrin®** (ibuprofen) and **Aleve®** (naprosyn). These medications should be used for moderate pain relief. Some indications are arthritis, muscle pain, fever and headache. **Motrin®** is usually taken three to four times a day and **Aleve®** is taken three times a day. **Aleve®** is easier on the stomach than **Motrin®**. Side effects are GI bleeding and stomach distress. Liquid **Motrin®** is available for people that cannot swallow pills, had a stroke or is used in addition to other prescription pain medications. I have recommended this for bone pain in cancer patients.

Tylenol® (acetaminophen) is the most used of the NSAID's. It is used by itself and in combination with prescription pain medications, flu combinations and pain and sleep combination products. Since the "Tylenol Scare" where the bottles were tampered with, acetaminophen has been on everyone's radar. November 12 Tylenol, radar contact, 2500 feet over the FDA. The doses of acetaminophen have become a controversy. Greater than 4 grams a day of acetaminophen could cause permanent liver damage that may lead to death. The biggest side effect of acetaminophen is liver toxicity. Patients that have taken too much need to get to the hospital where an antidote is administered before the damage is too great. We have a buffering system in our bodies that neutralizes the acetaminophen metabolite when it goes through the liver that causes problems. If that buffer system is overwhelmed with too much acetaminophen the toxic metabolite starts eating away at the liver. People who take too much may go into a coma.

Antidiarrheals

Imodium® (loperamide) is the product that is most used. It has opioid like effects but only in the intestine. Side effects include: abdominal pain, bloating and constipation. The FAA recommends only occasional use (1-2 times a week). If you are having bad diarrhea from a bad meal you may use probably more the 1-2 a day. As stated for cough and colds, if diarrhea is your problem, do not fly. The airplane makes a terrible toilet, like it makes a terrible classroom.

Kaopectate® and **Pepto Bismol®** are the same product now. The primary ingredient is bismuth subsalicylate. The is a chemical that is related to aspirin. These work OK, but I recommend **FiberCon®** or **Citrocel®**. If you want to go natural, try the BRAT(B-bananas, R- Rice, A- apple sauce, T-toast) diet. Yogurt replaces the good bacteria back into the hyperactive gut.

Cough and Cold Preparations

Nyquil® and **Dayquil®** are cough and cold products that have contained an antihistamine, decongestant, cough suppressant and analgesic. Products have included: pseudoephedrine (decongestant), dextromethorphan (cough suppressant), acetaminophen, antihistamine and previously alcohol. There are also many reports of people using too much dextromethorphan and getting hallucinations. Does this sound like something you want to be taking, fighting the runny nose and cough of a cold or flu while flying? Absolutely not, with a resounding no! These products just control symptoms. These symptoms, plus the medications are not going to make you a happy person at altitude, climbing, descending or landing. Take my advice, if you have a cold, do not fly until you feel back to normal. I have known multiple pilots who went up even 5 days post cold and suffered middle ear damage and severe headache. If taking **Dayquil®** it is said to hold off 12 hours after the last dose and **Nyquil®** about 60 hours.

If using these OTC's get better and DO NOT FLY.

Sleep

There are _**zero**_ OTC sleep medications that are on the FAA
Accepted Medication list. The only sleepmedications that I see is
Ambien® (zolpidem), **Lunesta®** (eszopiclone), **Restoril®**
(temazepam), **Rozerem®** (ramelteon) and **Sonata®** (zaleplon) for
sleep and that is by prescription only. There is a 24 hour wait after
Ambien® before flying. **Ambien®** is the most common sleeper
prescribed. Be careful if taking Ambien due to it's side effect, sleep
walking. People taking Ambien were gaining weight, even though
they were working out and eating right. What they did not realize
was they were sleep walking to the refrigerator and eating in their
sleep state. Upon waking up they saw how they were gaining
weight when they jumped on the scale, with no explanation.

FAA SLEEP AIDS

I. CODE OF FEDERAL REGULATIONS

**First-Class Airman Medical Certificate: 67.113(c) Second-Class
Airman Medical Certificate: 67.213(c) Third-Class Airman
Medical Certificate: 67.313(c)**

II. MEDICAL HISTORY: Use of sleep aids is a potential risk to aviation safety due to effects of the sleep aid itself or the underlying reason/condition for using the sleep aid.

All the currently available sleep aids, both prescription and over the counter, can cause impairment of mental processes and reaction times, even when the individual feels fully awake. (As an example, see the Food and Drug Administration drug safety communication on **zolpidem**.)

Medical conditions that chronically interfere with sleep are disqualifying regardless of whether a sleep aid is used or not. Examples may include primary sleep disorders (e.g., insomnia, sleep apnea) or psychological disorders (e.g., anxiety, depression). While sleep aids may be appropriate and effective for short term symptomatic relief, the primary concern should be the diagnosis, treatment, and resolution of the underlying condition before clearance for aviation duties.

Occasional or limited use of sleep aids, such as for circadian rhythm disruption in commercial air operations, is allowable for pilots and air traffic controllers. Daily/nightly use of sleep aids is not allowed regardless of the underlying cause or reason. **See Pharmaceutical Considerations below.**

PHARMACEUTICAL CONSIDERATIONS:

Because of the potential for impairment, we require a minimum wait time between the last dose of a sleep aid and performing pilot or ATCS duties. This wait time is based on the pharmacologic elimination half-life of the drug (half-life is the time it takes to clear half of the absorbed dose from the body). The minimum required wait time after the last dose of a sleep aid is 5-times the maximum elimination half-life.

The table on the following page lists several commonly prescribed sleep aids along with the required minimum wait times for each.

The medications below are by prescription only.

SLEEP AID WAIT TIMES		
Trade Name	Generic Name	Waiting Time before resuming pilot duties
Ambien	zolpidem	24 hours
Ambien CR	zolpidem(extended release)	24 hours
Edluar	zolpidem SL	36 hours
Intermezzo	zolpidem	36 hours
Lunesta	eszopicione	30 hours
Restoril	temazepam	72 hours
Rozerem	ramelteon	24 hours
Sonata	zalepion	6 hours
Zolpimist	zolpidem (oral spray)	48 hours

* NOTE: The different formulations of zolpidem have different half-lives, thus different wait times.

If you need to sleep no caffeinated products after 6 pm. Warm milk does really work and the caseins in milk will provide some nice dreams. Camomile tea with a dark room has been shown to work. **Benadryl®** is not a good sleeper and is contraindicated in the elderly. I will speak on Melatonin for sleep, in the supplement/herb paragraph.

Diet

Dexatrim® is a product that that advertises to give you the power to lose weight. There is no such medication that is the magic bullet for weight loss. **Dexatrim®** has caffeine, green tea extract, ginseng and DHEA in it. It has never been shown to cause weight loss. It has caused cardiac arrhythmias from the caffeine. I have seen this situation in the hospital and have had to code one patient in particular. He mixed it with other supplements with guarana and caffeine in them. Fortunately he survived after we resuscitated him and cooled his body to 33 degrees centigrade for 24 hours.

FAA

SECTION II, 3.7 SELF-MEDICATION (OVER THE COUNTER)

Non prescription medications are medicines that the patient can obtain or purchase that can be used to treat a condition that does not require   authorization by a physician or licensed medical practitioner.

DEFINITION OF OVER THE COUNTER SELF-MEDICATIONS

"Over the Counter" medications (OTCs) are legal, non-prescription substances taken for the relief of discomforting symptoms that may be in capsule, tablet, powder or liquid form. This could also include topical agents as well as agents that use a dermal delivery system (i.e. patch). In the Physicians Desk Reference for non prescription drugs (NP/PDR) and dietary supplements there are over 100 categories of medications that one can be obtained without a prescription. These, according to the NP/PDR treat conditions ranging from acne to wart care preparations. Also included in the NP/PDR are dietary supplements as well as diagnostics (i.e. pregnancy). Therefore, a person sometimes not only has the ability to treat but, in some cases, confirm a diagnosis that, heretofore, could only be made under the direction of a physician or licensed medical caretaker.

FAA Safe Medications (OTC)

1. **Advil®** (ibuprofen) antiinflammatory

2. **Alavert®** (loratidine) antihistamine

3. **Allegra®** (fenofenadine) antihistamine

4. **Aspirin** antiinflammatory

5. **Claritin®** (loratidine)

6. **Dayquil®** cold symptoms

7. **Dexatrim®** diet

8. **Imodium®** antidiarrheal

9. **Nyquil®** cold symptoms

10. **Prilosec®** (omeprazole) GI

11. **Sudafed®** (pseudoephedrine) decongestant

12. **Tagamet®** (cimetidine) GI

13. **Zantac®** (ranitidine)

14. **Zegerid®** (omeprazole + sodium bicarbonate) GI

15. **Zyrtec®** (cetirizine) antihistamine

Chapter 7.5
A Supplement on Supplements and Herbals

FDA and Supplements

Close your eyes. What do you see? Nothing! That is how the FDA feels on supplements and herbal products. If they cannot control the production of herbs and supplements, their stance will be to say, "we cannot say or stand behind products that are not proven to be effective with double blind randomized controlled trials." The best data base for herbs and supplements comes from **The Commission E Report** out of Europe. It is the German version of the FDA. Just like the FDA, there is controversy with them as well. Back in the 90's there were over 380 monographs looking at safety and efficacy of herbs. I have seen numbers that range from 10-50% of people in the U.S. have taken an herb or supplement at one time during their life. In a study done in Northwest England, looking at over 15,000 surveys showed that 12.8% of THE surveyed population took at least one herbal product. Users were more likely to be younger, female, white, owned their own home and use of herbs was not strongly associated with any health and lifestyle variables. There was no evidence that these folks substituted herbs for conventional medications. *Int J Vitam Nutr Res* 2004 May; 74(3):183-6. With us baby boomers getting into retirement age over 60 (myself) included, many highly educated people have sought other therapies.

FAA NOTHING, ZERO, ZIP AND NADA

This section is for <u>informational purposes only</u>. I want to do my due diligence to let you know there are herbals out there, that if taken will cause drowsiness or a change in mentation (thoughts and thinking). As we have discussed previously, these products could impair your judgement flying and are not to be taken before flight. I will be describing herbs that should NEVER EVER be used before flight.

Sleep

Valerian Root comes as both a tea, tincture and capsule. The tea smells like a dead animal has been taking refuge in your basement for a year. The tincture has about 30% alcohol in it and if you put it in hot water and do not let it steep you may be over the legal limits for alcohol. It has both sedative (sleepiness) and anxiolytic (antianxiety) effects. Back in ancient Greece and Rome it was described as a remedy for insomnia. Everyone knows of the Hippocratic Oath that physicians take to "do no harm". It was Hippocrates that described Valerian Root as a sleeper. It affects

GABA receptors which are the same receptors which **Valium®** works on. A systematic review and meta-analysis published in 2006 in the *American Journal of Medicine* concluded that, "The available evidence suggests that valerian might improve sleep quality without producing side effects." *Am J Med.* **119**(12): 1005-12. Side effects include: dizziness or drowsiness and as the label on the prescription bottle says do not take before driving or operating heavy or hazardous equipment, including an aircraft. I am adding **aircraft** to my new prescription side effect warning. **Melatonin** is a hormone found in plants, animals and microbes. Melatonin works on your circadian rhythms. Melatonin has been found in rice, tomatoes, corn and other fruits like cherries. Tryptophan is the parent compound that breaks down into melatonin in a four step process. Melatonin "hormone of darkness" is secreted in the brain by the pineal gland. The pineal gland is also a part of our sleep-wake cycle. High doses of melatonin could cause vivid dreams because it increases REM sleep. Melatonin was originally studied in people with jet lag and people working different shifts. It has a fast onset. Side effects include: drowsiness, nausea and irritability. Some folks have reported hang over sedation upon awakening. With this side effect profile and using it for sleep you can see, or should I say ZZZZZZ why this should not taken before flight.

Kava or **Kava Kava** is used as a sedative. It is reported to have calmative and relaxing properties without interfering with mental clarity. Kava's big use is for social anxiety. Its constituents are kavalactones and each has active properties. It also works on GABA, like valerian root does. The most common way to take it is as a tea. It can cause a very deep sleep. There is a potential side effect of hepatotoxicity with Kava Kava. The are several drug interactions with anticonvulsants, antianxiety medications like **Valium®,** diuretics and medications metabolized in the liver. The sedative and drowsiness effects are a concern for flying.

Chamomile tea also has sedative effects. It works on our new buddy GABA. The primary reason to have a cup of chamomile tea is to relax due to its sedative effects. Insomnia would be a reason to have a cup of tea. Just for all you blondes out there chamomile has been used to enhance the coloring of blonde hair.

Chapter 8
Pain

Pain in Latin (*peone*) means penalty. Pain in Greek(*poine*) mean punishment. Pain is very subjective. Each person has a different amount of pain tolerance. What is not known, except by a very few is that people have a different amount of pain receptors or receptors that pain medications attach too.

There are neuroreceptors, nociceptors and sensory inputs. There is local pain, musculoskeletal pain, neural pain, cerebral pain and bone pain, to name a few. There are even occasions of referred pain, where the pain may be happening in a different part of the body than where the pain is felt. There is even such a thing as phantom pain. I have seen multiple case reports, where an amputee will feel pain in the arm that was amputated.

From wherever the origin of the pain is, except things like headaches and migraines, pain will travel up the spinal cord into the thalmus. In the spinal cord there is a chemical called Substance P. It is also the place of the opioid receptors.

There are a couple of different kinds of medications for pain. The opioids, which include codeine, oxycodone, hydromorphone, morphine and Meperidine (Demerol®). All of the opioids are not on the FAA Acceptable Medication list. If you have a procedure, surgery or tooth extraction, you will probably be prescribed a medication with an opioid in it, such as **Vicodin®.** This medication has two different medications, actaminophen and hydrocodone. Taking the opioid medications is OK to control the pain, but not acceptable to take before a flight. If you need to take this kind of medication for pain control, do not fly. Once done with the prescription for the prescribed time, wait for at least 48 hours before flight.

The NSAID's work on inflammatory substances called prostaglandins. The most commonly used NSAID's include acetaminophen, aspirin, ibuprofen and naproxen sodium. There are many other NSAID's which are FAA acceptable. Their anti-inflammatory effects are well documented and very efficacious. Their indications for use includes high fevers, muscle and bone pain, predental procedures, moderate to severe pain and used in addition to other pain medications (aduvants). The biggest side effects with ibuprofen and naprosyn are GI bleeding and kidney dysfunction. These medications break down two enzymes. COX-1(Cyclooxygenase) that protects the stomach and COX-2 which is involved with inflammation (prostaglandins). Since they block COX-1 there is an increase in GI irritation. This is the reason why the person taking ibuprofen **(Motrin®),** needs to take it with food. **Celebrex®** is a different kind of NSAID. It is a COX-2 inhibitor. It will not breakdown the COX-1 that protects the stomach but will inhibit COX-2 that is causing the inflammation. It will not cause as much GI distress as **Motrin®**. The big controversy, as with other COX-2 inhibitors that have been taken off the market, is it may cause an increase in cardiac events this has not been proven. Everyone has heard about **Vioxx®**, which showed an increase in cardiac events like heart attacks. It created quite the stir, in that millions of people had gotten great relief from **Vioxx®**. The FDA took **Vioxx®** off the market.

There is a very unique medication, that is not included in the opioid category but works on the opioid receptor (weakly). It also works on serotonin and norepinephrine. The medication is called **Ultram®**. It is FAA acceptable and works very well for moderate pain.

For patients with osteoarthritis, **Tylenol®** is the number one choice of NSAID's. If the relief of pain is not seen with acetaminophen, the person is switched to another prescription NSAID like **Mobic®** (meloxicam).

Arthritis (Greek arthro - joint + itis - inflammation) is a joint disorder due to inflammation. There are many different kinds of arthritis. The most common kinds of arthritis is osteoarthritis and rheumatoid arthritis. Joint swelling and pain are the symptoms of arthritis. The major treatment modalities are the NSAID's. Acetaminophen is the medication of choice for osteoarthritis and

Ibuprofen or Naproxen Sodium is the medication of choice for Rheumatoid arthritis.

In Rheumatoid arthritis which is caused by an autoimmune process, the physician may have to add immune modulating medications. **Arava®** is an example of an immune modulator that works on DNA to prevent the development of future arthritis cells. **Enbrel®** is an injection that works on inflammation that is caused by high amounts of Tumor Necrosis Factor (TNF). **Humira®** is an injection also that also comes in an injection pen that works on TNF. Another oral immune modulator that is used in rheumatoid arthritis is **Rheumatrex.®** It works on RNA, DNA and other proteins to decrease the inflammation of rheumatoid arthritis.

<u>FAA</u>

Arthritis and Osteoarthritis and variants on PRN NSAIDS only.

Symptoms are well controlled with no persistent daily symptoms and no functional limitations

Issue – warn for changes in condition or additional medications use

Osteoarthritis, Rheumatoid Arthritis, and variants on medications other than NSAIDS

Review a current status report to include functional status (degree of impairment as measured by strength, range of motion, pain), medications with side effects and all pertinent medical reports

If airman meets all certification criteria – Issue.

All others require FAA Decision. Submit all evaluation data.

Initial Special Issuance - Requires FAA Decision Followup

Special Issuances - See AASI Protocol

Treating physician finds the condition stable on current regimen and no changes recommended.

Cause of Arthritis

None or mild to moderate symptoms with no significant limitations to range of motion, lifestyle, or activities

Acceptable causes are limited to:

Rheumatoid (limited to joint), psoriatic, or osteoarthritis

One or more of the following:

Oral steroid which does not exceed equivalent of prednisone 20 mg/day. Methotrexate, hydroxychloroquine (Plaquenil - see mandatory eye evaluation requirement below), NSAIDS.

Complete blood count (CBC) and complete metabolic panel

[ ] Within 90 days

[ ] Normal CBC, Liver Function Test, and Creatinine

FAA Report of Eye Evaluation

Form 8500-7 is required if hydroxychloroquine (Plaquenil) is used.

FAA Acceptable Medications for Pain

1. **Acetaminophen (Tylenol®)**

2. **Advil®** (ibuprofen)

3. **Amigesic®/Argesic®** (salsalate)

4. **Anaprox®** (naproxen)

5. **Ansaid®** (flurbiprofen)

6. **Arava®** (leflunomide)

7. **Arthrotec®** (diclofenac)

8. **Aspirin**

9. **Cataflam®** (diclofenac)

10.**Celebrex®** (celecoxib)

11. **Clinoril®** (sulinac)

12. **Enbrel®** (etanercept)

13. **Feldene®** (piroxicam)

14. **Humira®** (DNA monoclonal antibody, need to wait 4 hours before flight)

15. **Indocin®** (indomethacin)

16. **Kineret®** (recombinant receptor antagonist) injectable antiinflammatory

17. **Lodine®** (etodolac)

18. **Mobic®** (meloxicam)

19. **Nalfon®** (fenoprofen)

20. **Naprosyn®** (naproxen)

21. **Orudis® and Oruvail®** (ketoprofen)

22. **Relafen®** (nabumetone)

23. **Rheumatrex®** (methotrexate)

24. **Tordol®** (ketorolac) **<u>DO NOT USE FOR LONGER THAN 5 DAYS</u>**

25. **Ultracet®** (tramadol + acetaminophen)

26. **Utram®** (tramadol)

27. **Vimovo®** (naproxen + esomeprazole {proton pump inhibitor})

28. **Voltaren®** (diclofenac)

Chapter 9
Glaucoma

Glaucoma is an eye problem that is due to abnormal pressures in the eye. The elevated pressure of the fluid (aqueous humor) in the eye can damage the optic nerve and lead to blindness. The best term to describe glaucoma is "ocular hypertension." There are two types of glaucoma, open and closed angle. The angle is the area between the iris and cornea. Closed angle glaucoma comes on suddenly, is painful and if not taken care of quickly through surgery will lead to blindness. Open angle comes on gradually and folks with open angle may not even notice loss of vision until progression is significant. Hypertension is the silent killer and glaucoma is the "silent thief of sight."

Opthalmic solutions, eye drops will lower intraocular pressure. If the glaucoma patient is not compliant with their eye drops, vision loss will increase. **Xalatan®** is a prostaglandin that will increase outflow of excess fluid to decrease pressure. **Timoptic®** is a beta blocker that will decrease production of fluid in the eye. **Alphagan®** an alpha adrenergic that will decrease fluid production and increase outflow of excess fluid. **Pilorcar®** is a parasympathomimetic and will increase outflow of fluid. **Trusopt®** is a carbonic anhydrase inhibitor and will lower secretion of aqueous humor.

FAA GLAUCOMA MEDICATIONS

I. CODE OF FEDERAL REGULATIONS

First-Class Airman Medical Certificate: 67.113(b)(c) Second-Class Airman Medical Certificate: 67.213 (b)(c) Third-Class Airman Medical Certificate: 67.313(b)(c)

II. **MEDICAL HISTORY**: **Item 18.,d,** Medical History, Eye or vision trouble except glasses.

The applicant should provide history and treatment, pertinent medical records, current status report, and medication and dosage.

III. PHARMACEUTICAL CONSIDERATIONS

A few applicants have been certified following their demonstration of adequate control with oral medication. Neither miotics nor mydriatics are necessarily medically disqualifying. However, miotics such as pilocarpine cause pupillary constriction and could conceivably interfere with night vision.

Although the FAA no longer routinely prohibits pilots who use such medications from flying at night, it may be worthwhile for the Examiner to discuss this aspect of the use of miotics with applicants. If considerable disturbance in night vision is documented, the FAA may limit the medical certificate: NOT VALID FOR NIGHT FLYING.

FAA Acceptable Glaucoma Medications

1. **Alphagan P®** (brimonidine tartrate)

2. **Azopt®** (brinzolamide)

3. **Combigan®** (brimonidine + timolol)

4. **Cosopt®** (dorzolamide and timolol)

5. **Neptazane®** (methazolamide)

6. **Pilocar®** (pilocarpine)

7. **Timoptic®** (timolol)

8. **Travatan®** (travoprost)

9. **Xalatan®** (latanoprost)

Chapter 10
For Women Only
Estrogen

Menopause is not discussed extensively by the FAA, even though there are a significant amount of female students and pilots that are in their late forties or early fifties. This is sometimes not a happy time for women is this part of their life cycle. With the cessation of the reproductive fertility comes a decrease in hormones. The symptoms range from hot flashes, back pain, depression, irritability, depression, mood swings, inability to sleep and many others too numerous to mention. Back in the 80's, there were a huge amount of physicians prescribing estrogen replacement. It was felt that this would decrease osteoporosis and maintain a hormone level to help the maintain a more normal way of feeling. **Premarin®** (conjugated estrogen) is still being prescribed for menopause. The **Premarin®** name is derived from where the estrogens come from, **pre**gnant **mar**e's ur**in**e. There were studies that showed there was no change in osteoporosis rates and there may be an increased risk of DVT, stroke, breast cancer and endometrial cancer. Some of this data included the combination of estrogens and progesterone.

HORMONE REPLACEMENT THERAPY

I. CODE OF FEDERAL REGULATIONS

First-Class Airman Medical Certificate: 67.113(b)(c) Second-Class Airman Medical Certificate: 67.213(b)(c) Third-Class Airman Medical Certificate: 67.313(b)(c)

II.   **MEDICAL HISTORY:** Use of Oral or Repository Contraceptives or Hormonal Replacement Therapy are not disqualifying for medical certification. If the applicant is experiencing no adverse symptoms or reactions to hormones and is otherwise qualified, the Examiner may issue the desired certificate.

III.   **V. PHARMACEUTICAL CONSIDERATIONS**: See Medical History above.

Osteoporosis seems to always come up concerning what medications women should take that will be beneficial. This is because primary type 1 osteoporosis is seen in post menopausal women. Men get osteoporosis too.

Osteoporosis is the loss of calcium in the bones. It is a natural process of aging and primary osteoporosis type 2 occurs in equally in men and women. Osteoporotic patients have increased fractures and bone pain and in the elderly, that are frail may cause an increase fall risk. This could lead to the breaking of bones.

Biphosphonate medications help increase the bone matrix and allow calcium to be absorbed into the bone and increase bone density. Taking Vitamin D with calcium has never been proven to increase bone density.

Selective Estrogen Receptor Modulators are also used in osteoporosis in women. **Evista®** is an example. SERM's mimic estrogen and decreases risk of osteoporosis. Common side effects are hot flashes and cramps.

FAA

Menopause and osteoporosis is not even mentioned by the FAA, in the text of the AME.

FAA Approved Medications

1. **Actonel®** (risedronate sodium) - biphosphonate

2. **Boniva®** (ibandronate) - biphosphonate

3. **Evista®** (raloxifene) - SERM

4. **Fosamax®** (alendronate) - biphosphonate

5. **Miacalcin®** (calitonin-salmon) - nasal spray

6. **Premarin®** (conjugated estrogens)

7. **Reclast®** (zoledronic acid) biphosphonate

Chapter 11
For Men Only
Erectile Dysfunction (ED)

Besides all the other disease states we previously discussed, erectile dysfunction and low testosterone are the "for males only section".

Erectile dysfunction (ED) or impotence is the inability of maintaining an erection during sexual performance. Organic causes of ED are: cardiovascular disease, diabetes, neurological disorders (prostate surgery), hormonal effects and drug side effects. Psychological impotency is another cause in that psychological causes could cause impotency due to lack of self esteem. This plays upon itself because of a lack of performance on a continual basis leads to further depression. As a pharmacist, I am counseling all my male patients about their hypertensive medications. Most of them can cause sexual dysfunction, especially the beta blockers. The phosphodiesterase inhibitors (i.e.**Viagra®)** vasodilate which allows more blood into the penis which increases and holds the erection longer. The effects of the phosphodiesterase inhibitors could last from 24 to 72 hours. If an erection lasts for greater than 4 hours medical help should be received. Side effects include, hypotension, decreased vision, headache, nasal congestion and hearing loss. There is also available an injectable prostaglandin E1 that can be used before intercourse.

Low testosterone is another male malady that causes: low sex drive, difficulty in achieving an erection, hair loss, fatigue, lack of energy, loss of muscle mass, increased body fat, decreased bone mass and mood changes. There are testosterone gels and an underarm device that delivers the testosterone. Side effects include: dizziness, trouble sleeping, change in sexual desire, breast cancer in males, diabetes and obesity.

FAA Accepted Medications

1. **Androgel®** (testosterone gel)

2. **Caverject Impulse®** (injectable prstaglandin vasodilator)

3. **Cialis®** (tadalafil)

4. **Levitra®** (vardenafil)

5. **Viagra®** (sildenafil)

Chapter 12
Acne

Acne is a skin condition, usually seen in adolescence where an increase in testosterone causes pimples. There is an inflammatory reaction and redness is seen. Topical acne medications, antibacterial scrubs and oral antibiotics are the modalities used to treat acne. Acne's medical name is really scary, Acne Vulgaris. The person, as they get older will "grow out" of acne. Adults will sometimes still continue to get acne. If the acne gets really bad and all the other modalities have been tried, the dermatologists may choose an oral acne medication called **Accutane®** (isotretinoin). For an applicant, they must be taking Accutane® for at least 2 weeks. There are some night vision and psychiatric side effects that must be considered.

FAA ACNE MEDICATIONS

I. CODE OF FEDERAL REGULATIONS

First-Class Airman Medical Certificate: 67.113(c) Second-Class Airman Medical Certificate: 67.213(c) Third-Class Airman Medical Certificate: 67.313(c)

II. MEDICAL HISTORY:

Topical acne medications, such as Retin A, and oral antibiotics, such as

tetracycline, used for acne are acceptable if the applicant is otherwise qualified.

For applicants using oral isotretinoin (Accutane), there is a mandatory 2-week waiting period after starting isotretinoin prior to consideration. **This medication can be associated with vision and psychiatric side effects of aeromedical concern - specifically decreased night vision/ night blindness and depression.** These side-effects can occur even after cessation of isotretinoin. A report must be provided with detailed, specific comment on presence or absence of psychiatric and vision side-effects. The AME must document these findings in Block 60, Comments on History and Findings. Some applicants will have to be deferred. For applicants issued, there must be a **"NOT VALID FOR NIGHT FLYING"** restriction on the medical certificate. A waiting period and detailed information is required to remove this restriction. The restriction cannot be removed until **all** the requirements are met. See Pharmaceutical Considerations below.

III. PHARMACEUTICAL CONSIDERATIONS:

- Use of oral isotretinoin must be permanently discontinued for at least 2 weeks prior to consideration date (confirmed by the prescribing physician) and;

- Eye evaluation must be done in accordance with specifications in 8500-7 and;

- The airman must provide a signed statement of discontinuation that:

Confirms the absence of any visual disturbances and psychiatric symptoms, and:

Acknowledges requirement to notify the FAA and obtain clearance prior to performing any aviation safety-related duties if use of isotretinoin is resumed

Chapter 13
Summary

My mission and goal has been to give you, the pilot an idea of how medications work, the disease states they are used in and side effects. I love to teach folks about their medications and why they need to take them. This leads to increased compliance and better outcomes. The same holds true with my flight students. They need to understand why they are practicing a maneuver, instrument flying, going to a real grass airport, practicing crosswinds and to be able to get from point A to B with enough fuel, weather they can navigate in and to be able to land and stop on the runway.

Very few people get through life without a few maladies that affect their life. When something is not right you go to your physician. He or she may prescribe a medication for a chronic or short time. The medications have specific indications and come with side effects. The mechanism of action is the same and each person's physiology is a little different.

I am an evidence based pharmacist. I am part of a team of physicians that treat cardiology diseases. We use randomized controlled trials and evidence based guidelines to ensure the patients get the right medications. My hope is to provide you the best evidence based, safe and efficacious foundation I can to you, my fellow pilot.

It has been an honor and pleasure to share a little of my experience and knowledge with you. Each time I get up to teach or fly on my own, I am thankful for this privilege to aviate. I am in awe of the wonders of this earth. I am in awe on how airplanes fly. I am humble in my place to provide medication information to my fellow pilots.

My book is for information purposes on medications and to provide a reference source to you. This is NOT to replace your physician. It is also a reference to what is accepted by the FAA. The Aviation Medical Examiner (AME) is there to work with you and help you keep and get your medical certificate. I always keep in touch with my AME. He has helped me in multiple situations to help my students get their medical certificate. He is a fantastic resource and physician. Just like a great instructor, a great AME is priceless. The primary physician you go to for annual physicals and other disease states is a really important person to help keep you healthy. Having a great team of a primary physician and AME, will make your life outside and inside flying enjoyable and healthy.

Thanks a bunch.

Larry

References and Additional Reading:

1. Guide for Aviation Medical Examiners

2. AOPA FAA safe medications http://www.aopa.org/members/databases/medical/druglist.cfm

3. FAA Aeronautical Information Manual (AIM) – Chapter 8. Medical

Facts for Pilots, Section 1. Fitness for flight

www.faa.gov/air_traffic/publications/ATpubs/AIM/aim.pdf

4. Medications and Flying Brochure - FAA Publication

OK05-0005

(rev.6/10) www.faa.gov/pilots/safety/pilotsafetybrochures/media/

5. . "Sneezes and Zzzzs" - Aeromedical Advisory – FAA Safety

Briefing, March/April 2012

www.faa.gov/news/safety_briefing/2012/media/MarApr2012.pdf

6. http://www.diabetes.org/living-with-diabetes/know-your-rights/

discrimination/employment-discrimination/pilots-and-diabetes-

discrimination/faa-medical-

certification.html#sthash.t8AHs9XI.dpuf

Have a question?

Email Me at:

PilotLarry7@gmail.com

INDEX By Chapters

Clinoril® (sulinac)……………………………………..8

Combigan® (brimonidine + timolol)……………………….9

Combivent® - (ipratropium + albuterol)………………….6

Coreg - (carvedilol)………………………………….2

Cordarone® and Pacerone® - (amiodarone)……………….5

Cosopt® (dorzolamide and timolol)……………………….9

Coumadin® - (warfarin)……………………………….5

Corgard and Corzide - (nadolol)……………………….2

Clozaril (clozapine)………………………………….1

Cozaar (losartan)…………………………………….2

Crestor® (rosuvastatin)……………………………….4

Cymbalta (duloxetine)………………………………….1

Dayquil®……………………………………………7

Desyrel (trazodone)………………………………….1

Dexatrim®…………………………………………7

Diabeta and Glynase - (glyburide)……………………….3

Diovan (valsartan)…………………………………….2

Diuril - (chlorthiazide)……………………………….2

Dramamine (dimenhydrinate)……………………………..1

Dyazide - (hydrochlorthiazide + triamterene)………………..2

Dyrenium - (triamterene)……………………………….2

Edarbyclor (azilsartan)……………………………….2

Effient® (prasugrel)………………………………….4

Eliquis® (apixaban)………………………………….5

Exforge (valsartan + amlodipine)……………………….2

Elavil (amitriptyline)………………………………….1

Effexor (venlafaxine)………………………………….1

Enbrel® (etanercept)………………………………….8

Eskalith (lithium carbonate)……………………………1

Evista® (raloxifene)………………………………….10

Feldene® (piroxicam)………………………………….8

Firmagon (degarelix)………………………………….1

Flovent® - (fluticasone)……………………………….6

Fosamax® (alendronate)……………………………….10

Haldol (haloperidol)…………………………………..1

Humira® (DNA monoclonal antibody)…………………………8

Hydrodiuril - (hydrochlorthiazide)…………………………….2

Hyzaar (losartan + hydrochlorthiazide)………………………..2

Indocin® (indomethacin)……………………………………8

Glucophage and Glumetza XR - (metformin)………………..3

Glucotrol - (glipizide)………………………………………3

Humulin, Novolin and Novolog- (insulin)……………………3

Imdur (nitroglycerin)……………………………………..1

Imodium®……………………………………………….7

Inderal - (propranolol)………………………………………2

Invokana (canagliflozin)……………………………………1

Janumet - (sitagliptin + metformin)………………………….3

Januvia - (stiagliptin)…………………………………….3

Kerlone - (betaxolol)………………………………………..2

Kineret® (recombinant receptor antagonist)…………………..8

Klonopin (clonazepam)……………………………………1

Kombiglize XR - (saxagliptin + metformin)……………………3

Lantus - (insulin glargine)…………………………………3

Lescol® (fluvastatin)………………………………………..4

Levitra® (vardenafil)………………………………………11

Lipitor® (atorvastatin)………………………………………4

Livalo® (pitavastatin)………………………………………4

Lodine® (etodolac)…………………………………………8

Lopid® (gemfibrozil)………………………………………4

Lovenox® - (enoxaparin) anticoagulant injection)………………5

Lovaza® (omega 3 fatty acid)……………………………….4

Levatol - (penbutalol)………………………………………2

Levemir - (insulin)…………………………………………3

Lexxel and Plendil - (felodipine)……………………………2

Lotrel - (amlodipine + benazepril)……………………………2

Lopressor and Toprol XL- (metoprolol)………………………2

Librium (chlordiazepoxide)…………………………………1

Lotensin (benazepril)……………………………………2

Loxitane (loxapine)……………………………………1

Luvox (fluvoxamine)……………………………………1

Mavik (trandolapril)……………………………………2

Maxide - (hydrochlorthiazide + triamterine)………………2

Mevacor® (lovastatin)……………………………………4

Mexitil® - (mexilitene)……………………………………5

Miacalcin® (calitonin-salmon)……………………………10

Multaq® - (dronedarone)……………………………………5

Moduretic - (hydrochlorthiazide + amiloride)……………………2

Mobic® (meloxicam)………………………………………**8**

Mykrox - (metolazone)……………………………………**2**

Monopril (fosinopril)……………………………………2

Micardis (telmisartan)……………………………………2

Minipress - (prazosin)……………………………………**2**

Nalfon®(fenoprofen)……………………………………8

Naprosyn® (naproxen)……………………………………8

Neptazane® (methazolamide)………………………………9

Nexavar (sorafenib)……………………………………1

Niaspan® (niacin extended release)………………………4

Norpace® - (disopyramide)……………………………………5

Norvasc - (amlodipine)……………………………………2

Normodyne - (labetalol)……………………………………2

Nyquil®………………………………………………**7**

Omacor® (omega 3 fatty acid)……………………………4

Orudis® and **Oruvail®** (ketoprofen)……………………8

Pamelor (nortriptyline)……………………………………1

Paxil (paroxetine)……………………………………1

Pilocar® (pilocarpine)……………………………………9

Plavix® (clopidogrel)……………………………………4

Pravachol® (pravastatin)……………………………………4

Pradaxa (dabigatran)……………………………………**1**

Premarin® (conjugated estrogens)………………………10

Prilosec® (omeprazole)……………………………………7

Onglyza - (saxagliptin)……………………………………………3

Precose - (acabose)…………………………………………3

Prednisone® - (prednisone)………………………………………6

Prinivil and Zestril (lisinopril)…………………………………2

Prinizide (lisinopril + hydrochlorthiazide)……………………2

Procardia - (nifedipine)……………………………………..2

Proventil® - (albuterol)…………………………………………6

Qvar® - (beclomethasone)…………………………………………6

Questran® (cholesteramine)…………………………………………4

Reclast® (zoledronic acid) bisphosphonate……………………10

Relafen® (nabumetone)…………………………………………8

Remeron (mirtazapine)…………………………………………1

Revlimid (lenalidmide)…………………………………………1

Rheumatrex® (methotrexate)………………………………………8

Rythmol® - (propafenone)…………………………………..5

Sinequan (doxepin)………………………………………………1

Sectral - (acetbutolol)……………………………………..2

Serevent® - (salmeterol)…………………………………………6

Seroquel (quetiapine)……………………………………………1

Serzone (nefazodone)……………………………………………1

Spiriva® - (tiotropium)…………………………………………6

Sudafed® (pseudoephedrine)………………………………………7

Sular - (nisoldipine)…………………………………………………**2**

Surmontil (trimipramine)………………………………………1

Sutent (sunitibib)………………………………………………1

Symlin - (pramlintide)……………………………………………1

Symbicort® - (budesonide + formoterol)…………………………6

Tagamet® (cimetidine)……………………………………………7

Takeda - (alogliptin)………………………………………………1

Tambocor® - (flecainide)…………………………………………5

Tarceva (erlotinib)………………………………………………1

Tenormin - (atenolol)……………………………………………2

Theodur® and Uniphyl® - (theophylline)…………………………6

www.ingramcontent.com/pod-product-compliance
Lightning Source LLC
Chambersburg PA
CBHW072152090426
42740CB00012B/2233